GEO. A. PFLAUM, PUBLISHER, INC.

exploring the film

WILLIAM KUHNS & ROBERT STANLEY

Library of Congress Catalog Card Number: 68-9282

Photographs taken during the filming of the motion picture "Bonnie and Clyde" appearing on pages 35, 37, 40, © 1967 by Warner Bros. Pictures, Inc.

Pflaum Staff For Exploring the Film

Editorial: Marlene Shebu
Art: Ned Ostendorf, Rita Mathews
Production: Ken Langosch, Cathy Ebert
Special Photography: Paul Tucker, Alan Oddie

First Printing, August, 1968

Second Printing, October, 1968

AUTHORS' NOTE

Seeing a movie is, of course, far different from reading about a movie. We believe that seeing and knowing the movies themselves are more important than knowing many factual things about film history, techniques, and the like, for in the one case the knowledge is part of living, whereas in the other the knowledge seems merely academic.

As a result, the emphasis in this book has been upon duplicating—as far as possible in a book—the experience of seeing and knowing good films. Movies are made to be seen, not read; and though much of this book is print, it too has been made to be seen, just as much as read. To this purpose the book has a design which we hope you will find lively, and gives more emphasis to understanding the experience of a film than to the specific techniques that went into the making of the film. There are no questions at the end of chapters; there isn't even an index. We don't think their omission will hurt your appreciation of the book. It's a book to look at; and there's a great Spiderman comic if, in spite of all our efforts, things get a bit tedious.

A number of people have contributed their generous time and help to this book. We would like to thank especially Mr. Art Brown at Brandon Films, Inc.; Charles Boos, Millie Purwin, and Rick Thompson at Contemporary Films, Inc.; James Lysyshyn and Denis Belleville of the National Film Board of Canada; the Museum of Modern Art, New York, especially Miss Marilyn Goldin of its Film Stills Archive; Alan Twyman, Jr. of Twyman Films, Inc.; Alan Oddie for help with the photographs and text; Stan Lee of Marvel Comics; and Karen Zekowski, for her unflagging work in typing the manuscript.

William Kuhns / Robert Stanley

foreword

Why teach or study motion pictures? Isn't the commercial film entertainment, and little else? To many in schools it appears a far-fetched conception to think of this motion picture in connection with education.

Yet, it is surprising that so few good textbooks on motion pictures are available to high school students and teachers. The creation of such volumes lags far behind the absorption and interest of teen-agers in films. We live in a world of instant communication, with the film as its center, and yet most of us are only beginning to comprehend its implications and its promises.

So EXPLORING THE FILM is welcome. William Kuhns and Robert Stanley know their subject and present it attractively, with insight and meaning. The teacher will find it is an excellent resource and guide; students will find that it sheds illumination on a medium which pre-occupies so much of their time.

Think of these statistics. It is estimated the average young person being graduated from high school today has seen 250 commercial feature films in theaters, and the equivalent of 7,500 two-hour feature films on television, for a total of 7,750 features. The time that the graduate has spent in the classroom in 12 years is, by comparison, the equivalent of 5,400 feature films, or 2,350 fewer.

Anything of such pervasive interest to young people is of course the proper concern of education. Many secondary schools today have courses on motion pictures. The vaster number does not. To the school system which wishes to keep abreast of its students and with the external world in all its aspects, the film offers stimulating and productive prospects. EXPLORING THE FILM can be a good partner in this educational adventure.

Kenneth Clark,
Executive Vice President,
Motion Picture Association of America,
June 1968

contents

INTRODUCTION: WHY STUDY MOVIES?

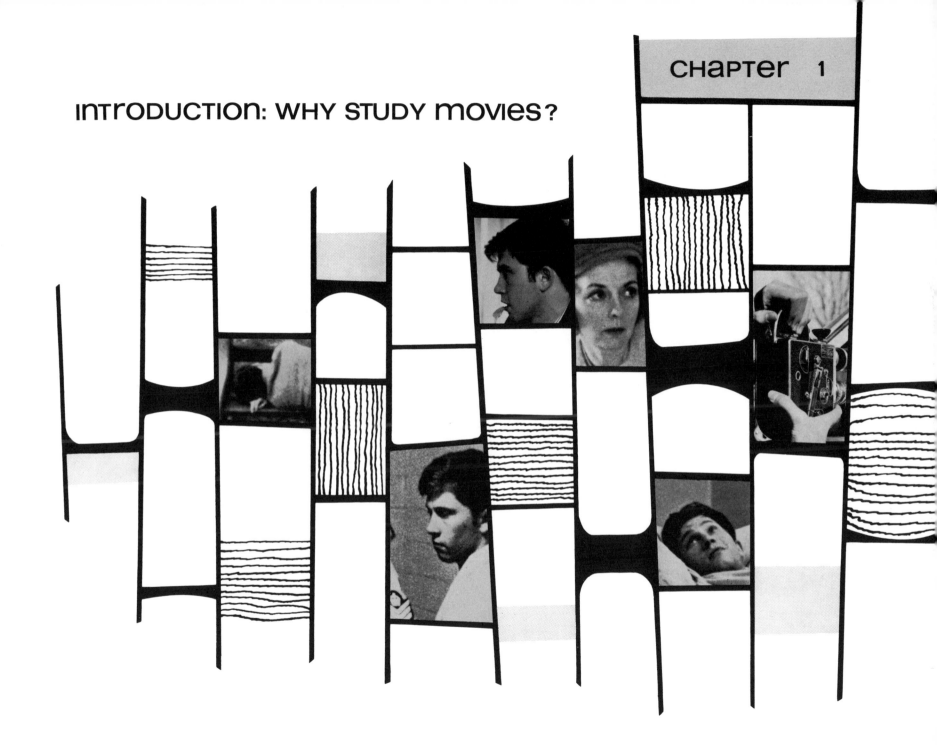

CHAPTER 1

At the opening of NOBODY WAVED GOODBYE, a boy and a girl are tumbling gaily alongside each other in a cemetery. They seem unaware of being surrounded by images of death; they are enjoying each other too much, playing, laughing, kissing. In the background there is heard an old English folk tune, "Love is Tender":

The river is wide, I cannot see
Nor do I have wings to fly
Give me a boat that can carry two
And both shall row, my love and I.

Peter Kastner, of the National Film Board of Canada production NOBODY WAVED GOODBYE

The boy is Peter Mark, a bright, rebellious high school senior; the girl is Julie, a classmate. Despite the joys of frolicking in a graveyard, the two are doing it on school time. And at supper that night, Peter watches his mother explode because the principal had called. Peter finds his mother's badgering and his father's quiet restraint too much to bear. He lunges from the house, grabbing the keys to his father's new company car — a long, powerful convertible.

He and Julie are stopped by the police: both for speeding and for running two red lights. And Peter has no license. At this point Peter decides that authority can only mean tyranny, and he refuses to bow to tyranny. He decides to move into his own apartment, gets a job at a parking lot, and struggles to earn enough money to escape from town with Julie. Soon he begins short-changing customers in order to acquire more money sooner; but he still doesn't have enough, and the temptation to steal money and a car becomes too attractive. Peter doesn't wait. When Julie, on the highway, learns that the car is a stolen one, she insists that Peter turn around or let her out. He lets her out, only to gasp at the discovery that she is pregnant. But he won't turn back, and Julie refuses to

join him. As Peter drives into the night, the theme returns, "Love is Tender" :

> *When love is young, then love is fine,*
> *Just like a jewel when first it's new*
> *Loves grows old, and it waxes cold*
> *And fades away like the summer dew . . .*

On a first viewing, NOBODY WAVED GOODBYE is a rich and powerful movie. But much of the power of the film, and its ability to communicate important ideas about young people in today's world, come from the expert handling of filmic material — the techniques the film maker uses.

For example, the director (a Canadian, Don Owen) did not give the actors a script. He explained the situation to them and what was to happen — then let them act each situation out naturally. The effect is a startling realism, more reminiscent of "Candid Camera" than of most movies. Another example: the way in which the director attempted to describe the tension in Peter's life between freedom and the constraining forces of society. The opening sequence, Peter and Julie's tumbling around in a cemetery, is a free, exciting happening; and the freedom is brought out forcefully by the contrast between the vitality of two young people and the stiffness and deadness of the tombstones that surround them. A later sequence, depicting Peter and Julie on a boat in the park, gives the same glorious sense of freedom; here the canoe's freedom to move in any direction on the smooth lake underscores the liberation that Peter and Julie feel.

Most of the film (and especially the second part) is not about freedom, however; it is about constraint. Peter and Julie are denied freedom by their parents, their school, society, and ultimately by themselves. NOBODY WAVED GOODBYE succeeds because it conveys this deprivation of freedom with subtlety and depth, always using the language of film.

Scenes from the National Film Board of Canada production NOBODY WAVED GOODBYE

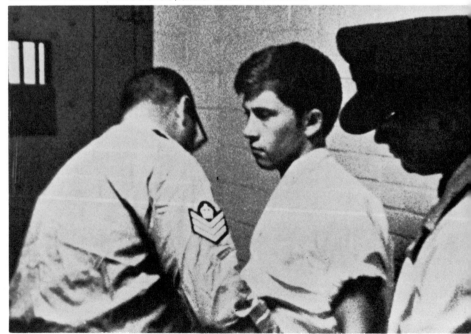

Charmion King, Peter Kastner, and Julie Biggs in scenes from the National Film Board of Canada production NOBODY WAVED GOODBYE

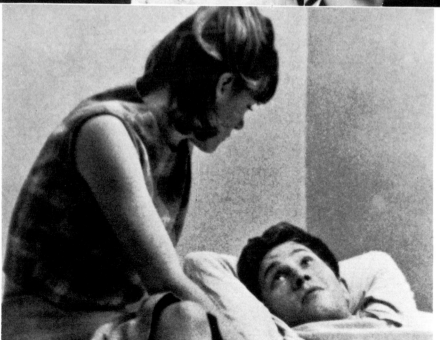

What is tragic about NOBODY WAVED GOODBYE is that many viewers are not sensitive to the real language of film and miss much of what the movie is attempting to communicate. They see the story, they come to like the characters, but they are never intrigued by the provocative questions raised. They enjoy the music, but do not listen to the caustic comment contained in the words. They are impressed by Peter's and Julie's love for each other, but do not notice the subtle way in which Peter is using Julie to achieve his own freedom. They have looked at the film, but they have not really seen the film.

In a film like NOBODY WAVED GOODBYE there are many things to look for: for example, the way in which faces express vivid feelings; the contrast between persons and places (as with Peter and Julie in the graveyard); the use of song to heighten feeling and at the same time comment on the fact that these joys cannot last. Not that looking for these things becomes a hard, laborious effort. Active involvement in film-watching adds to the enjoyment and appreciation of a movie. It won't detract from it.

Books and movies are very much unlike, but book-readers and film-viewers share an important characteristic. A reader whose vocabulary is broad, who can follow descriptions and ideas intently, who can be highly critical of the elements of a novel will obviously get more out of reading a book like HUCKLEBERRY FINN than a lazy, half-asleep reader who is simply following the plot. The same with a lively film-viewer. If he enters the theater or turns on his TV set and makes an effort to watch, he will probably get more out of what he sees. It's all very much a matter of looking — and of knowing what to look for.

The purpose of this book on films and the work you will be doing in "film study" is simply to enable you to look and then to see. David Wark Griffith, a great, early American film maker, once summed up his purpose in directing films by saying, "My purpose is above all to make you see." The final purpose of this study of films is to make you see.

Looking (and seeing) is an experience all its own; it is very difficult to talk about it. Consequently, this book includes all sorts of visual materials — still shots from movies, simple photographs, line drawings. See what you can make of these; they may be helpful in making you familiar with the visual language you will be working with for the next few weeks. Visual language is vital for communicating many experiences that simply can't be expressed verbally: how to describe a young girl's joyous face in words? But what you can do with a movie camera . . . !

It isn't enough, however, simply to read about this visual language: you must look at movies and television shows and try to see what's there. You will discover much of what you saw (but didn't recognize as being important) when you discuss the film afterward. Discussing a good movie is half the fun of watching it. Discussion also gives you a good indication of how much you did see.

A good discussion demands a number of things. Some helpful guidelines for a lively discussion might be:

1. Listen to what each person has to say.
2. Relate each comment to the remarks of the previous speaker.
3. Emphasize the way in which the camera communicates.

There is more to learning the language of film, however, than can come simply through watching and discussing movies. Somewhere along the line you're going to feel the itch to get behind a camera yourself, to make your own movie. As with any language, you really haven't learned visual language until you've used it.

Making a film is simple. It's inexpensive, and it's very, very possible: even if you don't have a camera and have never held anything bigger than a Brownie shutterbox. A four-minute color film on 8mm. can be made (i.e., filmed, developed, and edited) for only a few dollars. The items for which the Hollywood studios run up the biggest expenses are really free if you know how to get them: light, ideas, talent, settings.

The final section of this book deals with making films. As soon as you feel the urge to try your hand at film making, read it. You may already feel the itch; read it now. But don't let the opportunity to make a film pass you by — even if it's only a mock cigarette or automobile commercial. Some of the most imaginative short films in recent years have been coming out of the universities. And the competitions for high school films (Kodak sponsors one annually) have shown that high school students can do highly creative and polished work with a camera. Try it.

Movies have always been fun. Studying how they communicate to us doesn't mean that they will lose any of the fun; quite the contrary. For the better we know the language they are using, the better we can understand, appreciate, and enjoy them. (That's the whole point of studying any language: it enables you to listen to it and speak it more accurately.) And the more sensitive we can become to the human values communicated in movies — which is perhaps the final and most important reason.

But don't take my word for it. See for yourself.

WHAT'S IN A MOVIE?

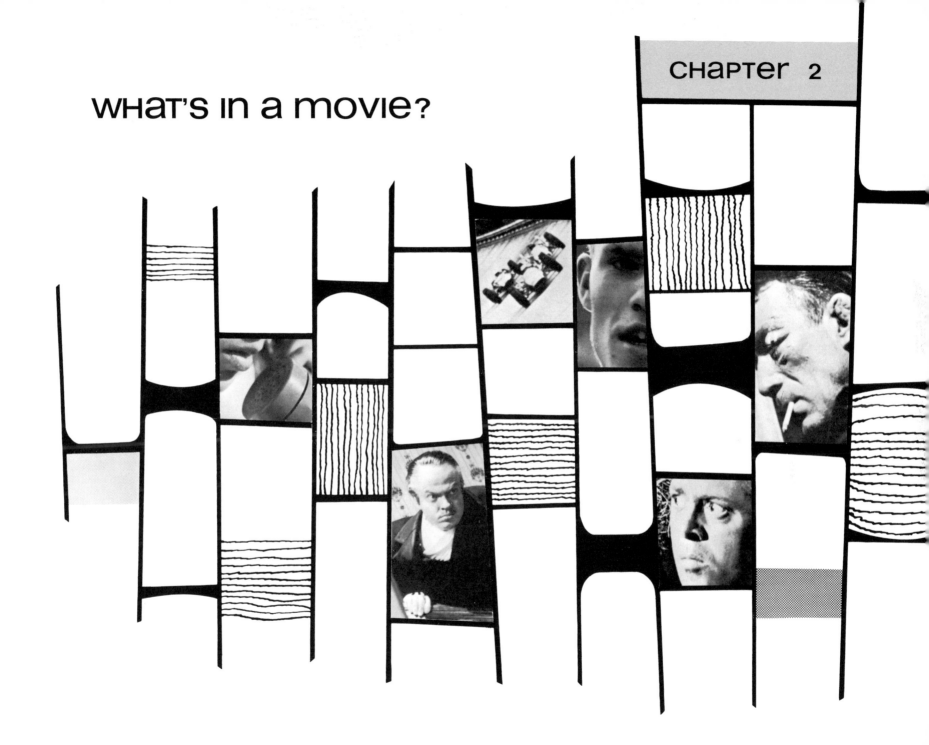

CHAPTER 2

Why do people like movies? Ever since the turn of the century when two-minute sequences were shown in circus sideshows and later in nickelodeon palaces, movies have attracted crowds.

The most obvious fact about movies—and perhaps the most satisfying—is that they

They are alive. The cars in GRAND PRIX surround and terrify us as they catch the road's curve or spin for a second out of control. The gripping horror of the shower murder scene in PSYCHO is paralyzing. The beautiful moments in AN OCCURRENCE AT OWL CREEK BRIDGE in which the prisoner breathes, hears birds sing, and catches the glimmer of sunlight on the dewy leaves show how lifelike and lyrical a film can become. The fast, impact-filled editing of a TV series like "Mission: Impossible" can heighten tension and give a very simple plot tremendous suspense.

A good film never stops moving. Even if th
camera is held still, the subject should be alive–
not simply sitting down and talking, but alway
revealing himself through movement: a nervou
flitting of hands, a stolid, gritting assurance at th
helm of a ship. In the Italian film LA STRADA,
simple young girl named Gelsomina becomes th
traveling companion of a brutish circus strongma
Zampano. Nowhere does the film stop. Whethe

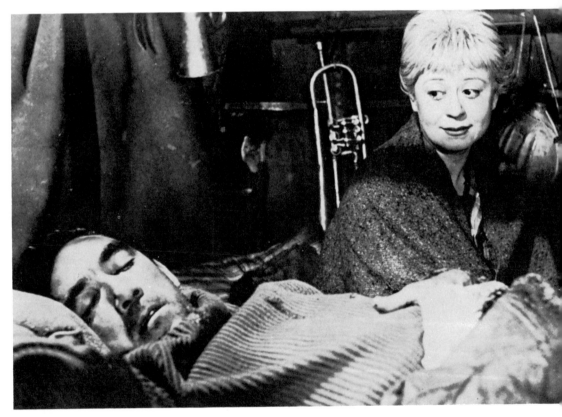

Scenes from the Trans-Lux release, LA STRADA, directed by Federico Fellini. Courtesy of Museum of Modern Art/Film Stills Archive

is Gelsomina's pathetic pacing, Zampano's iron-
nding, or the little wagon traveling down the
ad (*la strada* is Italian for "the road"), the film
ays constantly alive and makes its characters
me to life. Out of this life there emerges a poi-
ant statement about human loneliness and human
mmitment. But the statement is powerful and
sturbing only because the film is filled with life,
th the rhythms, gestures, and expressions of
wer-class Italians.

There are a number of reasons people go to the
ovies. Sociological studies indicate that they go to
cape their normal, humdrum existence and to
perience a life more exciting than what they're
ed to. They go because they like the actors or be-
use they heard a film had a good story. But more
portant than why they go to movies is why
ople are satisfied with movies. And since the
ys of Charlie Chaplin, it has been fairly evident
at people are happy with movies charged with
e.

Films can come to life in a variety of ways.
ovement doesn't simply mean that Superman
mes swooping through an open window or that
unds go bounding through the underbrush after
ox. The camera can provide the movement. In
e recent film, for example, a group of girls are
king at a circular table; to accent the spirit of
ls, the camera is slowly moved on a wagon
ound the table, always catching a different face.
e camera can move horizontally (the term is
anning") and disclose a sweep of mountains or
ity skyline. It can tilt (move up or down) to
phasize the power of a gunman or the dwarfish
e of his opponent. The camera can zoom in on a
e or a man holding a gun in an apartment win-
w or move quickly from a large scene to a very
icentrated part of the scene.

ANGLE

16

Camera movement, however, is always limited—and never as powerful as the movement of the subject. There is yet another form of movement, the background. In the beautiful Russian film THE BALLAD OF A SOLDIER, a young soldier and a girl sit in a moving freight car of a train from which they and the film viewers see the passing fields and trees. The scene is glorious; the peace the couple experience is captured in their repose against the simple beauty of the countryside that whizzes by. Again, movement speaks with a directness and an immense power to evoke feeling.

In the following chapters, the elements that go into the making of a film will be discussed—the equipment, the men, the process. Here, however, it is enough to mention that a film lives or dies by its use of motion. Movement is at the heart of any good motion picture, and the lack of movement is often the main reason for a poor one.

Is it simply motion that captivates an audience in a theater, however? The ways in which films affect audiences are still largely unknown. The sociologists and psychologists have done some research and have reached some conclusions, but for the most part the effects of movies upon their audiences are still unclear.

There are two things of which we are fairly certain: that the experience of a movie in a theater is a very intense and all-encompassing experience; and that in viewing a movie, the viewer comes to identify himself with characters on the screen. Both facts can help us to understand better what happens when someone goes to the movies.

enes from the National Film Board of Canada production THE RUNNER

One of the most obvious and important differences between a movie in a theater and the same movie on TV is the size of the screen. But coupled with the size of the screen there is another difference: the environment. An environment is the surroundings in which a person finds himself: anything from an elevator to a mountainside. The environment of which a person is conscious in a theater is solely the screen; its size helps it dominate his attention, and the rest of the theater is darkened. In other words, seeing a movie in a theater means experiencing the film as an environment—a totally surrounding experience. This experience of film as environment is carried further in Cinerama, where the screen literally surrounds the viewer. In the rapids sequence of HOW THE WEST WAS WON, the person in the theater actually feels he is *in* the river, swirling with the raft and debris.

Obviously there is a severe contrast between film as environment and film as it is found on TV. Watching television, you are focusing your eyes on a relatively small area in your house. And you can rarely forget your environment: the dog will fall asleep under the screen, someone might walk through the room, and there are always commercials to remind you of the Coke in the refrigerator. But in a theater there is little to distract your attention from the screen, and when you are distracted, usually you feel more annoyed than when distracted watching TV. In other words, the film in a theater provides a total environment, whereas the TV film is only part of a larger environment.

Metro-Goldwyn-Mayer, Inc., HOW THE WEST WAS WON. Courtesy of Museum of Modern Art/Film Stills Archive

The second point involves the bond that exists between the characters on the screen and the audience. In THE GREAT ESCAPE, a number of GIs are being kept in a tightly guarded concentration camp near Holland. Although conditions at the camp are not impossible, the soldiers cannot stand being cooped up without making an effort to escape. Three tunnels are begun; but before they are completed, one is discovered. All of the energy of the soldiers goes into finishing the second tunnel: reinforcing the walls, disposing of the dirt, and finally making arrangements for civilian clothes and identifications for the men who will slip out. The evening of the escape we follow every step with suspended breath. The first man's discovery that the tunnel's exit still lies yards short of the woods is frightening enough. But to watch each man emerge clumsily from the hole and dash toward the woods—with the tower guards and their spotlights only a short distance away—turns the theater itself into that very tunnel and the perilous, grassy spot outside the wall. When the spotlight finally glares down on one of the escaping prisoners and the sirens wail, the viewer feels *he* has been caught —that all of *his* efforts have been ruined.

EVEN SO

scene from the National Film Board of Canada production PH

Film has a marvelous capacity for arousing the sympathy of the audience. The short film PHOEBE depicts a sixteen-year-old girl throughout the day on which she has discovered her pregnancy. Phoebe's dark, sickened mood dominates the film, and soon we are made to share her gloom. The techniques for conveying her mood to the audience are simple: we follow her mind flashing backward and forward in time and are caught in her rhythm of thought, her bitter sadness. A pained sympathy for Phoebe is unavoidable. Techniques can be highly effective in building up sympathy. In the opening four minutes of REQUIEM FOR A HEAVYWEIGHT, we do not see a clear shot. We see one fighter in a boxing ring nimbly sparring and packing heavy punches; then, spiralling downward, we see the swirl of lights, the referee's long, dipping arm, and finally hear the roar of the audience. We watch lights blend and glare as two men jostle through the crowds to the dressing room. Only in the hall outside the dressing room does the camera focus and show us, in the mirror, the bruised, swollen face of Mountain Rivera, the story's hero. From this moment on, we feel what Mountain feels—as when he touches his image on a fight poster outside the arena and is hurt by the recognition that his boxing career is finished. The rest of the film establishes a tremendous sympathy with Mountain—and successfully, because the opening sequence (known as "subjective camera") has given *us* the experience of losing a championship boxing match. We have stood (and fallen) in Mountain's shoes; we cannot help but feel deeply with Mountain as the film progresses.

Without this ability to arouse strong identification with people, movies would not be as popular as they are. We want to identify, we want to feel other people's glory or elation, sadness or pain. It is the well-made movie that enables us to do this. The use of such techniques as flashbacks, subjective camera, close-ups, and a monologue on the sound track that speaks the mind of a character can establish a strong rapport between audience and character.

This rapport is not always desirable, as in A MAN FOR ALL SEASONS, where we are forced to separate ourselves from Sir Thomas More to sense the contrast between his heroic stature and our lack of heroic stature. But generally sympathy serves an important function in the watching of a motion picture.

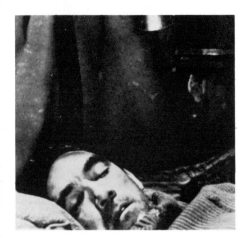

There is a great deal more that can be said about the experience of a film than that it becomes a total environment and that it can create a strong bond of sympathy with a character. Most of the other points, however, are simply consequences of these two facts. If we feel a burning desire after seeing GRAND PRIX to get into a powerful racing car and tear down a highway at 150 miles per hour, it proves only that the impact of the totally encompassing visual experience and the strong feelings shared with characters have made a powerful impression upon us. And it is a good thing to be aware that movies *can* make very strong impressions on us, since numerous movies don't reflect life very honestly, and the strong impressions they leave us with may be more illusory than real. Girls aren't as accessible (to most men) as they are to James Bond or to Napoleon Solo. It is a pity for anyone who thinks they are.

Movies have always fascinated audiences, and they will no doubt continue to fascinate audiences. Probably the most basic source of their fascination, as we learned, lies in the fact that they *move* —they are more lifelike than painting, books, sculpture, even dance. But movies also fascinate us because they can draw us into a different, totally fresh environment—and can make us feel strongly with an actor or actress. As long as they continue providing this freshness and these feelings, there is little doubt that they will last.

THE SHAPING FORCES OF FILM Language

Any language — English, French, German — is not simply born; it is shaped over a long period of time. And one can understand a language a little better in seeing what shaped it.

The same is true of the language of film—although in a different way. We can never fully understand how films speak to us until we see how they operate and how they were shaped. This chapter will explore the devices that make film language possible—camera, film, projector—and the very early history of the moving-picture camera. Understanding both the mechanics of film and the history of film can be a great asset in comprehending film language more clearly.

An 18th century engraving of a magic lantern.

fig. 3.

A typical E. R. Muybridge photographic sequ

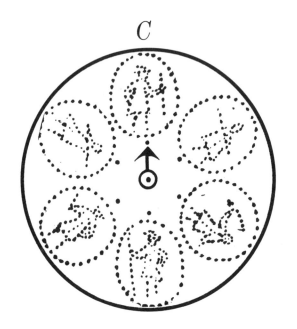

C

A Kinetoscope parlor, 1895. Courtesy of Museum of Modern Art/Film Stills Archive

Charlie Chaplin, SHOULDER ARMS. Courtesy of Museum of Modern Art/Film Stills Archive

A movie happens. When Charlie Chaplin in POLICE is trying to break into a house window with a chisel (but no hammer), a policeman comes up from behind. Chaplin doesn't notice the cop but goes on with the chisel, quite unsuccessfully. The policeman, getting a kick out of his efforts, hands Charlie the hammer. Charlie doesn't use it on the window, though; he bops the policeman on the head. Then, sure that the cop is out cold, he tries the door—which is open.

Just like every other sequence in a movie, this sequence *happens*. Charlie Chaplin—with a hammer, a cane, or the burdensome soldier's equipment in SHOULDER ARMS—makes things erupt on the screen right in front of us. With the single exception of television (either live or videotape), no other device can make life happen again so realistically. And most of the things seen on television have first been filmed. The movie is the art that is always alive, always happening. But how?

19th century engravings of E. J. Marey's camera.

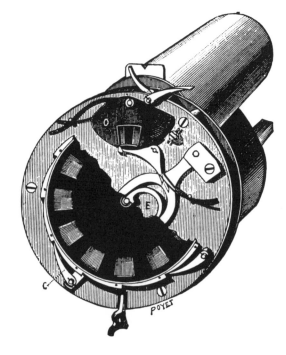

Chronophotograph by Marey, 1882.

A moving picture works because of two things: a camera can capture stopped, small fragments of motion, and our eyes cannot tell the difference between a succession of these fragments and the real thing. The camera, first of all, is built like the human eye—it permits light to enter and to register what is outside. Inside the camera a long, narrow strip of sensitive, coated celluloid runs down through the lens opening. Usually a battery-powered motor pulls the film through at about the rate of a foot a second. Each rectangular slide on the film (called a frame) catches a bit of motion, slightly different from the frame that went be-

fore it. In the standard 16mm. cameras used for newsreels, 24 frames move through the lens *each second*. This means that a frame catches someone in motion for about 1/24 of a second.

When we watch a movie, then, we are not really seeing motion: we are seeing consecutive shots flashed so quickly onto a screen that we think they are in motion. Our eyes are weak when it comes to spotting quick changes in motion. Through a curious thing called "persistence of vision," we tend to continue seeing what we just saw. Close your eyes quickly, and you will continue seeing this page.

R. W. Paul's Animatograph. Courtesy of Museum of Modern Art/Film Stills Archive

After a light is flashed on and off suddenly in a dark room, one continues to see the light—for a longer time than it was on.

Movies work because of the persistence of vision. When the eye's grasp of each frame overlaps onto the next, and this happens again and again and again, the final effect is like seeing actual motion. People move naturally, smoke wisps upward, streams flow: motion has been reproduced—or seems to have been.

Technically, then, the entire production and viewing of a movie rests on two basic principles: that a camera can catch successive, tiny fragments of motion; and that the human eye will see these fragments as a continuous moving picture.

Historically, it took a long time before these principles could be discovered and developed into the motion picture. By the middle of the nineteenth century, still photography was fairly well developed. And some scientists knew of persistence of vision. A number of photographers were fascinated by the possibility of catching moving objects with a camera.

The most important pioneer in taking a succession of pictures of an object in motion was Eadweard J. Muybridge. By the 1870's, when he was a well-known photographer, Muybridge was commissioned to photograph a racehorse owned by the governor of California. He was to discover whether at any moment all four of the horse's hooves were off the ground. By using a 1/1000-of-a-second shutter speed, he succeeded. But the problem of catching a horse in motion fascinated him, and soon he had lined up a battery of a dozen cam-

...as to record almost simultaneously the movement ...f a horse. When the pictures were developed, they ...owed the horse in various stages of motion. Look-...ng at a set of his pictures today, they resemble ...ills from a film sequence more than they do a ...uccessive series of single photographs.

Muybridge never went further than his multiple ...amera technique. But he opened the door; within ...0 years after Muybridge, a number of men, many ...nspired by his achievement, attempted a machine ...hat would catch on a long strip of film the suc-...essive shots which Muybridge had captured with ...a number of cameras.

Many tried; none—at least yet—succeeded. Some ...f the most notable efforts were made by E. J. ...Marey, who developed a gun with a circular rotat-...ng film; Augustin le Prince, who built a camera ...ith numerous lenses; and Wordsworth Donis-...horpe, who attempted to switch single plates ...uickly enough to catch successive fragments of a ...moving object.

A number of men were responsible for impor-...nt contributions to what we know today as the ...movie camera. Thomas Edison and a Scottish as-...stant, W. K. L. Dickson, developed a movie cam-...ra that is the basis of the contemporary camera. ...sing film 35mm. wide (which is still the stan-...rd size for theatrical showings), Edison and ...ickson ran the film through the camera at 46 ...rames, or pictures, per second. They did not, how-...er, go further and develop the projector; they ...uilt a viewing machine, called the Kinetoscope, ...n which a coin had to be inserted and which would ...un the film before the single viewer's eye.

Robert W. Paul in England recognized the in-...erent limitation of Edison's Kinetoscope: it could ...how films only to one customer at a time. Paul ...eveloped a projector and gave the first public ...emonstration of it in 1896. At the same time in ...rance the Lumière brothers opened the first ..."movie theater": an exhibition of films that they ...d made and for which they charged a fee. Their ...ms were usually about 50 feet in length and ...ntered around subjects like "Changing the Guard ...t St. James' Palace," and "Turning out the Fire ...ngine at Southwark."

One of Muybridge's motion studies. Courtesy of Museum of Modern Art/Film Stills Archive

Edison Studios, 1912. Courtesy of Museum of Modern Art/Film Stills Archive

By the end of the century numerous men were following the Lumière brothers in shooting and projecting films. The popularity of these showings was proof that later efforts to develop a motion picture industry would be successful. People wanted movies. They were fascinated by movement —even if it was only the movement of a train pulling into a railroad station.

The history of the development of the motion picture shows that a number of men struggled over a number of years to make moving pictures *work*. Even before they had been invented, movies were wanted. The still photograph, in itself a remarkable invention, was not enough: people wanted to see photographs resemble life in every way—and the most outstanding way was movement.

It took less than a decade for the novelty films shown in the Lumiere exhibitions to become an important form of public entertainment, with serious, lengthy films attracting large audiences. And it would be only a few more years before film making became an industry—indeed, in countries like America and Germany, a major industry. People craved films. They found in films something they could not find in books, music, or drama. And it would take the combined efforts of numerous men to find what people wanted in films and to develop it. But that is another history: the history of film itself.

Thomas A. Edison's RECORD OF A SNEEZE
Courtesy of Museum of Modern Art/Film Stills Archive

HOW a FILM IS made

Obviously there is more to a finished movie than what it takes to pull a long strip of film through a box. Somehow the studios that made films like CLEOPATRA and THE SOUND OF MUSIC managed to spend tens of millions on each film. Where did all the money go? To put the question in a different way, what is involved in the making of a movie?

A great deal is involved. Hundreds of men—at times thousands—take part in the production of a major film. Huge studios must be outfitted; sometimes immense properties in the local region where the film is shot must be rented and set up. A good percentage of a film's budget might go into costumes and settings. Then there are the technical costs of shooting, developing, editing, and reproducing the film. But the costs of making a film are all accepted as part of the process, part of the long, involved effort of putting life on film just as the film maker wants it.

Who, first of all, is the film maker? In a Hollywood production, where major decisions are made by half a dozen different people, who can rightly be called the maker of a film? In the involved film making process, so many people make important decisions that it is difficult to label any one man as film maker.

Generally, though, one man plays the most important role in shaping a film and can rightly be called the film maker: this is the director. The director is usually involved in every step of the film making process, from the writing of a film script to the final editing of the movie. As his name suggests, he "directs" the action, the expressions of the actors, the positioning and movement of the cameras. While the film is being shot, his word is final. Many directors reserve the right to control the editing of the film after it is shot.

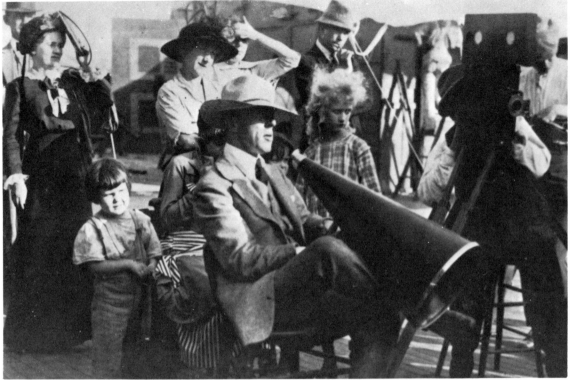

Director D. W. Griffith. Courtesy of Museum of Modern Art/Film Stills Archive

Director Donald Owen, Julie Biggs, and Peter Kastner of National Film Board of Canada production NOBODY WAVED GOODBYE

At the center of the film making process, th
there is the director. Yet his relation to the fi
remains that of a member of a team to a j
which, essentially, the team is to do. The film
rector (with a few exceptions—and most of th
directors in Europe) does not totally control wh
happens in the film, as the artist totally contr
what happens on his canvas. The director simp
has *more* control than anyone else on the fi
making team.

A film does not begin with the director. It b
gins with the combined power of a good idea a
the money to translate that idea into a film. Go
ideas are available in many places; but the kind
money needed to put these ideas onto film is n
Indeed, usually it will be made available for a fi
only by professionals trained in making money c
of films.

So a film begins, realistically, in the hands o1
film producer who has money—let's say a Hol
wood producer, head of a large studio. (The ki
of money needed to make a commercial film
usually prohibitive for individuals: production
an average commercial film runs close to a milli
dollars.) Suppose a producer has just read a nov
and is excited by its possibilities as a film. He co
sults with a few other studio members, perhaps
prospective director and writer. They might li
the idea of working the novel into a film. T
writer and publisher of the book would be co
tacted, and—usually at impressive expense
rights secured for the studio to make the nov
into a film.

The producer's next job is one of aligning t
talent he will need to make the film. Very oft
his first concern will be for a starring actor. N
all producers are happy about the idea, but t
starring actor's image and popularity have a gre
deal to do with how well a film succeeds. At t
same time, the producer will find a director—pe
haps the most important decision he will make
determining the outcome of the film. Some dir
tors, like David Lean (BRIDGE ON THE RIVER KW
LAWRENCE OF ARABIA, DOCTOR ZHIVAGO) ha
chosen their own material.

Another important appointment that the producer makes is that of an associate or assistant producer. The associate producer has a big job: he must overlook all of the technical, financial, and artistic arrangements involved in the making of a film. Many of the key figures involved in the film, including, sometimes, the director and the writer, will be chosen by the associate producer.

With, finally, a producer, a director, and an associate producer, the basic plans for the making of a film can be outlined. A writer is chosen; he usually works in collaboration with the director, who gives him a clear idea what kind of development the film should have. While the writer is at work on a suitable script, the associate producer makes arrangements for casting actors to fill the roles. An assistant director is assigned to work with the film's director: this man is responsible for freeing the director, wherever possible, to work without worries about set design. He will obtain another lens for the cameras or solve the thousand other small problems that arise.

The early steps in the making of a film are generally hectic ones. Copies of the finished script are sent to the various departments of the studio (art department, paint, carpentry, electrical, etc.) for cost estimates and to assist them in preparations. During these preparatory months the director confers frequently with the various people he will be working with: the set designer, the cameraman, the actors. Set design is extremely important in a film, especially for directors attempting to create highly realistic scenes. The set designer must keep in mind not only the effects that the director wants (for example, in a terror sequence, strong shadows against dark walls) but also the needs of the cameraman (who must have proper light and the right angle to shoot from) and the sound engineer (who must record effectively in the set).

Usually someone is assigned to compose or find music for the film, most of which is added after everything else has been finished. The music must fit the scenes, and therefore the director of music cannot do much until he knows exactly how long each scene will be.

In the meantime, under the director and an assistant called the casting director, actors have been chosen to fit the major and bit parts in the film. A shooting script, with a page for every shot, has been prepared; the director, cameraman, and editor will work from this. The shooting script is arranged into a shooting schedule, so that the director, technicians, and cast know ahead of time what scenes will be shot when. A film is practically never acted out and shot in the sequence in which it appears on the screen: one of the last scenes might be shot first, and one of the early scenes shot last.

The actual work of shooting the film is lengthy, involved, and—as anyone involved in film making knows — somewhat nerve-racking. The preparations for each shot are innumerable: lights must be arranged, sound equipment prepared, cameras set up, the setting perfected, the actors ready. Before the cameras roll, the actors will rehearse their lines several times until the director is satisfied. Then the "shot": the point from which the camera begins and at which it ends. Usually there are a number of "takes," meaning that a shot is taken several times until the director is happy with one.

© 1967 by Warner Bros. Pictures, Inc.: actor-producer Warren Beatty, BONNIE AND CLYDE

20th Century-Fox, DESERT VICTORY, produced by the Film Units of the British Army and R.A.F. Courtesy of Museum of Modern Art/Film Stills Arch

The enormous work that goes into one shot accounts for the relatively small amount which seemingly is accomplished in one day of making a film.

1 day = 3 minutes

In the making of a carefully handled film, if one day yields three minutes of a final film, it can be considered a successful day.

As soon as the film has been shot, it is sent to the laboratories where it is developed, and temporary prints (or "rushes") are struck from the negatives. These prints are viewed by the director and producer, and perhaps the main actors for approval before the set is disassembled or before the crew moves to a different location.

When all of the shooting is finished, the editor takes all the prints and makes what is called a "rough-cut." This is a collection of all the shots joined together in the proper order. The director and producer view the rough-cut and decide whether they will need to reshoot any sequences. If nothing needs to be reshot, studio work on the film is finished. Sets can be taken down and actors can be released.

The film is now ready for editing. The editor, often working closely with the director, begins with the assembled rough-cuts. His big job is to determine when and how shots should begin and end. The editor controls a great deal of the final film: he can determine the tempo, the clarity of story progression, and many of the effects of a good film. If the editor is given a well-shot film to work with, his contribution can be highly creative.

When the editor is finished and the film has been sent through the labs, the final stage of production — the music — is begun. The musician may have written his own score or he may have borrowed it; but it is important, for dramatic effect, that the music be synchronized with the action. Usually while the musician is working on the score, other technical assistants — especially the sound engineers—finish their part of the work. Early preparations are also probably being made for promotion of the film.

A scene from the National Film Board of Canada production LONELY BOY

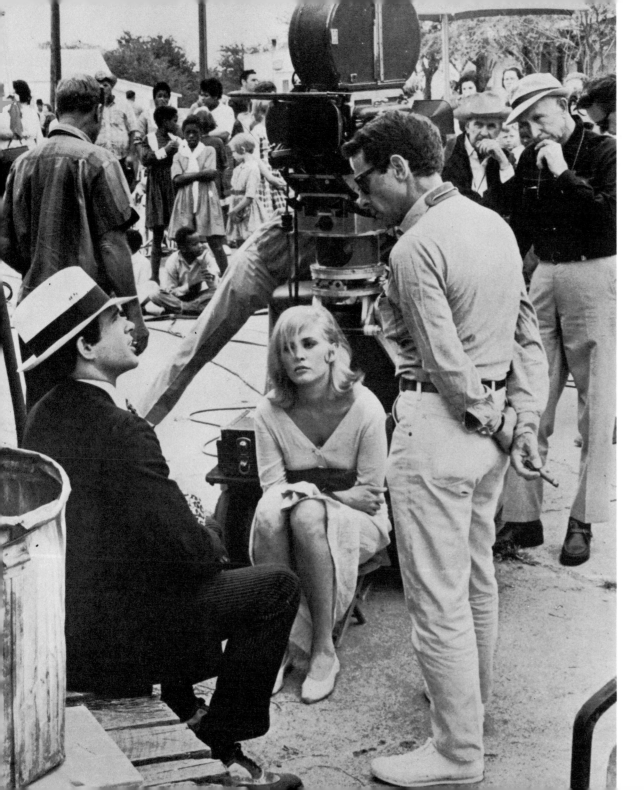

The final film, with music and sound, will b
viewed by the director and producer; if they ar
satisfied with it, hundreds, perhaps thousands, o
copies will be made for distribution throughout th
country and overseas.

This account is far too brief to give a total ide
of the efforts that go into the making of a film
While a movie inevitably goes through the step
mentioned above, these steps may not follow th
same order. And they may not always involve di:
ferent people. Many directors have written thei
own films; many have edited their films. Som
movies are made with almost all of the editin
work done on the shooting script—before a scen
is shot by the cameras. Some movies, on the othe
hand, leave a tremendous amount of work to th
editor. There are no rigid rules on the process o
making a film.

This pattern of film making is not followed, o
course, in the making of documentaries, or nor
fiction films. A documentary (which attempts t
depict real events and real people) depends on th

Canadian film artist, Norman McLaren

...ay things already are: no writer or director can
...onstruct sets or prepare actors for a documentary.
...he process of making a documentary will be
...eated at length in Chapter 11.

The important thing to recognize about the pro-
...ess of making a film is that all the complex efforts
...hould lead to a single, well-organized film. If the
...nal movie is weak in any one aspect (for instance,
...lumsy lighting), the whole suffers—despite, for
...xample, excellent acting, good settings, and effec-
...ve editing.

As mentioned earlier, throughout the making of
... film no one plays a more critical role in the
...haping of the final movie than the director. The
...ign of a really good or great director is that his
...lm bears his personal signature: he can be iden-
...fied by it. Anyone who has seen many Alfred
...itchcock films knows what to expect when he goes
... see a new Hitchcock movie: it will be charged
...ith suspense built through such external effects
... music and setting. It is above all the director of
... film who "makes" the final movie. Most failures
... well as successes can be traced to him.

The process of making a film may seem so complex as to discourage amateur film making. It shouldn't. The things that cost the major studios the most money are precisely the things which a resourceful student with a camera can get for nothing: actors, a good setting, light, props. Some very good, even some great, movies have been made on shoestring budgets. And millions and millions have been poured into supercolossal flops. The important thing about making a film is the desire to communicate effectively in visual language. All else is secondary. Indeed, if anything besides this desire becomes primary (the best example is money), it is doubtful whether true visual communication will be the result.

so, communicate!

A CHAIRY TALE, a National Film Board of Canada production

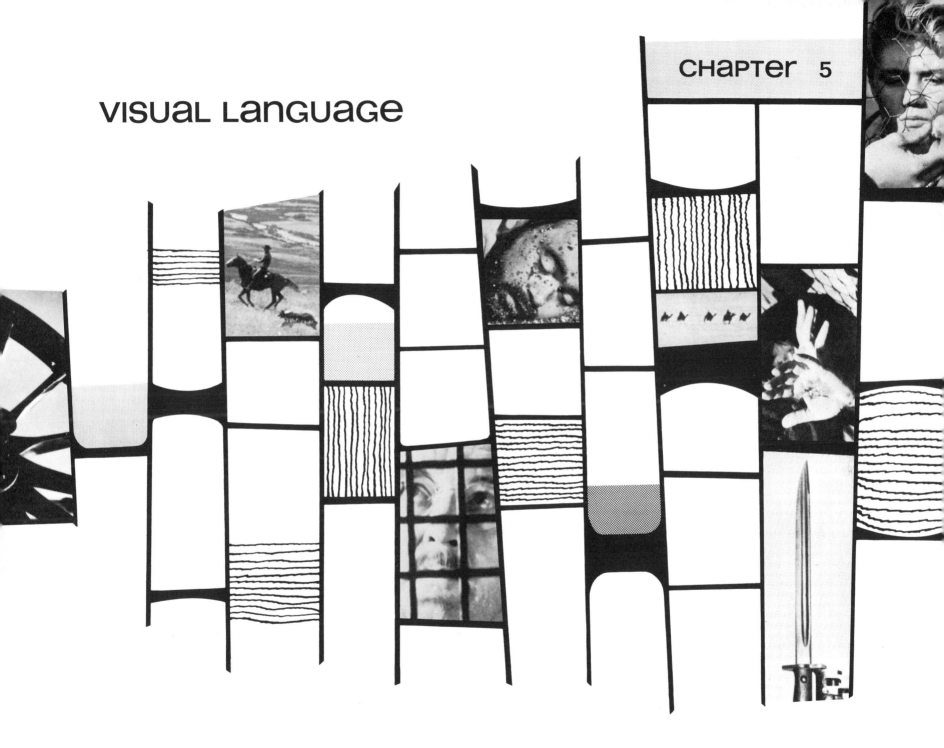

VISUAL LANGUAGE

Film, as we have said, is a language all its own. Through its own visual vocabulary and grammar, it speaks and can be powerfully expressive. The long, winding road in LA STRADA brings grief and sympathy to a lonely girl; the roaring Formula 1 cars in GRAND PRIX convey an excitement that seems to put the viewer in the race itself. Nobody who has seen many movies would deny that they can be highly expressive. But in attempting to understand the *way* in which they are expressive, it is essential to understand some of the basic elements of film language.

The film maker is usually in the same position as the poet: he must say something, and he can say it either in a trite, prosaic way, or with great imagination. Suppose we are watching a film in which a man is about to be shot by a firing squad. We have sympathized with this man for a good part of the movie, and even though he must die, the film maker wishes to use his death to make us feel much more strongly for his cause. How will the cameras take the shooting? From a single camera position, set back so that we can see the whole event? This would generally be a prosaic, ineffective way of communicating the horror of the execution. Suppose instead the camera moved vigorously from the victim's eyes to the glowering face of the commander, from the victim's nervous hands to the cocked guns of the soldiers. Finally an arm is raised, fingers tighten on the triggers, and a volley of shots rings out. The camera, set on the ground, watches the victim slump to the dust, dead. Then a final, penetrating look at the soldiers and the commander whose blank faces suggest the absence of any feeling about what they have done.

Film language will be successful only when it is highly expressive—only when every shot not only *shows* what is happening, but to some extent also reveals the meaning of what is happening. In THE LONELINESS OF THE LONG DISTANCE RUNNER, for example, a young man has been arrested and sent to a Borstal House, or reform school, in England. The young man does not simply resent authority; he feels contempt toward anyone's efforts to curb his freedom. Two stills from the film, reproduced here, suggest his feelings. In the headmaster's office, he breaks the forward, silent gazes of the other two boys to glare insolently at the headmaster. Standing next to the fence, we can see that he is closed in; but the low camera angle makes us look up to him, admiring him, and recognize his superiority over his enclosure.

Fundamentally, a film is expressive in three ways: through the language of its picture, the language of its motion (especially editing), and the language of its sound. These are not three different languages, but all are part of film language. This chapter will explore the ways in which the picture itself can be expressive.

The picture, it must be remembered, is always present and yet is never present. It is always present in the sense that there is always some sort of a picture on the screen. But it is never really present in the way that a painting on a wall is present: totally accessible. In a film a picture may flash by only for a second. The term "moving pictures" is an appropriate one, and generally the picture can rightly be made dependent upon the motion. Although it is important that the picture be expressive, it is *more* important that the movement dominating a film be expressive.

There is something of a golden rule governing expression in an individual shot of a film—a rule that can perhaps be broken, but which it is generally best to follow. If a film's basic purpose is to express or to communicate, the film maker should set up his shot so that the object or situation he is trying to depict will be best represented. In other words, *each shot should concentrate on the features of its subject that best bring out the inner nature of the subject.*

Some examples: An Italian film THE BICYCLE THIEF described a man and his son searching throughout Rome for a stolen bicycle. At one point they are shown in pouring rain, with a camera angle that looks down at them—evoking a mixed sympathy and pity. In the Russian classic OCTOBER (also known as TEN DAYS THAT SHOOK THE WORLD) a number of men and women are pushing a heavy cart. The director spent hours before he decided how to set up his camera: the tilt he finally achieved enabled him to bring out the heroic strength demanded of the people to move forward.

The golden rule of visual, pictorial expression is, then: each shot should bring out the inner qualities of the subject matter.

THE BICYCLE THIEF, directed by Vittorio de Sica. Courtesy of Museum of Modern Art/Film Stills Archive

How, though, is this done? There are numerous ways in which the film maker can be expressive with his picture, but five are used most frequently and deserve some attention.

1: FRAMING

One of the most fundamental differences between the way our eyes see normally and the way they see in a movie theater is the rectangular border that frames a film. No film escapes this border. But this rectangular shape—within which the movie must fit—is really a great asset to the film maker, for it enables him to isolate figures and places and attract attention to them. The effect of a frame will always be to set apart and distinguish what is inside. Especially on the regular-sized screen, with its capacity for focusing our attention on a single small thing, the framing of the screen can concentrate on ordinary things and thereby give them added beauty: the glitter of water in a creek, a flash of sun through branches, a buoyant face.

Larger screens—notably Cinemascope and Cinerama—lose the capacity of attracting our attention to a small thing. But they have the advantage of handling large action and immense settings in a

20th Century-Fox release, NINE HOURS TO RAMA: a Mark Robson production ·

© 1965, The Landau Company and Herbert R. Steinmann, THE PAWNBROKER with Rod Steiger

convincing way. On the one hand, the stretching desert and the bands of marauders in LAWRENCE OF ARABIA were not fit for a small screen; on the other hand, the close-up love scenes of Anthony and CLEOPATRA were not fit for the large screen. No love scene can look totally serious or convincing when a leading star's nose stretches for some 12 feet across the long, long movie screen.

The point about the screen as a form of framing is, then, important: a large screen is suitable only when the subject is right. The same goes for a small screen. Sometimes seeing large-screen, panoramic movies put on a TV screen can be frustrating—like watching a football game through a peephole.

There is another kind of framing that the film uses, known as interior framing. This is the conscious effort of the film maker to set up his shots so that the characters and action are framed within the total picture. This conscious device of framing can make very effective statements about the situation in the film. At the opening of the Canadian short YOU'RE NO GOOD, the boy Eddie is standing across the street from a parked motorcycle. Before we learn for certain how he feels about the motorcycle, we are given a strong visual hint: we see the motorcycle framed by his arm. The suggestion of possession mingled with the distance of the motorcycle from Eddie provides an extremely effective visual statement.

There is another, final way in which framing can be used in a film—a method found more frequently in very recent movies and television shows. This is the method of breaking the screen in two or three parts and showing different (or the same repeated) action in the different frames. When he made GRAND PRIX, John Frankenheimer broke up the screen frequently—sometimes to show the racing cars multiply, sometimes to show a driver's face speaking to another driver of a speeding car. The method can be effective, but it is always artificial and should not be overused.

MAN OF ARAN, produced by Robert Flaherty, 1934.

2 PLACEMENT

Whenever we see a picture on a screen, we are looking at the subject the way the camera looks at it. And whatever attitude the camera takes toward the subject—whether of admiration or disdain, indifference or sympathy—we take on the same attitude. In the opening sequence of MAN OF ARAN, we are introduced to the family of a fisherman living off the coast of Ireland; to present the wife as a courageous and heroic woman, the cameras look up at her as she climbs across the gnarled rocks. With the sky behind her, the woman appears powerful and impressive—the suggestion of a camera angle.

The two major ways in which camera placement can affect the shot we see are the camera's distance from the subject and the angle with which it looks at the subject.

Camera distance is an extremely important aspect of film expression. Almost no films are made with one constant camera distance: the camera is always shifting from far away to nearby, to very close up to the subject. The basic camera distances and their general uses are as follows:

Long-Long Shot: Taken at a great distance, perhaps 40 feet or more. Usually used for opening shots or perspective shots, it is the best type of shot to show a major event (such as a battle) or a terrain (such as a forest).

Long Shot: Taken at a distance, but not so great as a long-long shot. It is also used for perspective.

Medium Shot: Taken at about 6 feet from the subject; usually a person standing upright can be completely seen in the shot. The medium shot is the standard shot in most films.

Close-Up: A concentration of the camera upon a face or some other feature—perhaps a hand or a foot. The close-up concentrates the viewer's attention on one thing and can be extremely impressive, for the viewer becomes deeply involved in the action.

Scenes from the National Film Board of Canada production THE RUNNER

Close Close-Up: An almost microscopic view of some feature: for example, an eye or a thumb taking up the whole screen.

Of course, the actual shots used in films are most often a combination of two of these types of shots; but this is the basic pattern.

In the making of a film, it is important to vary the types of shots, because the undue repetition of any one kind of shot deadens the effect of the film. At the same time, appropriate shots should be used at appropriate moments. Most scenes open with a long shot or a long-long shot—what is called an "establishing" shot. This shot gives the viewer a knowledge of where he is and what he can expect. To catch the exact response of a woman to a threatening phone call, the director will not use a long shot or even a medium shot: the close-up would be most effective here.

The distance of the shot can be expressive not only on the basis of what information the film maker wants to convey about the subject, but also through the psychological effect of a certain distance. Distances speak. If two men are arguing bitterly, they will probably stand a good 3 to 4 feet from each other—perhaps more. If, on the other hand, they are trying to discuss a business proposition, they will stand much closer. The executive who likes to keep people aware of his position usually sits at an enormous desk (much larger than he needs) that keeps visitors 10, perhaps 15 feet from him. In a similar way the camera often uses its distances from the subject to express its attitude toward the subject. A medium-long shot of a raving maniac may be more effective than a close-up if the director wants to keep us aware of a certain distance. The use of close-ups can make us feel close to the characters and more sympathetic to them. The exclusive use of longer shots can sometimes convey the same kind of distance the executive with his large desk might want to convey.

Camera angle is the second aspect of camera placement. There are three standard angles: low (viewing the subject from beneath), level, and high (viewing the subject from above). Again, there are countless variations to the possible camera angles that can be achieved in making a film. The angle from which a shot is taken can make a strong impression on the viewer. A shot in CITIZEN KANE had the camera placed low. Not only is the character Kane made awesome and strong by the low camera angle, but also the backdrop of his own face on a rally poster gives him added strength, added power.

CITIZEN KANE. Courtesy of Museum of Modern Art/Film Stills Archive

One of the best sources of dynamic pictorial angles is the comics. The artists designing comics have often sought the best position from which to state the action in a panel. Consequently, the angles they use are often highly original and highly expressive. In the *Spiderman* comic included here, what are some angles that strike you as being especially strong and expressive, and why? Would these be possible in a film?

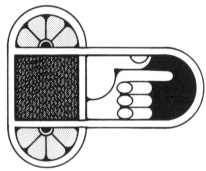

Sergei Eisenstein, a great Russian director, once said that for every object in every situation there is the perfect angle from which to shoot it. His own films illustrate this restless quest for the most suitable camera angle — as we can see by examining some shots from his movies. A creative and lively use of camera angles can give a film not only greater intensity, but also an increased capacity for expression.

Where camera distance and camera angle are used imaginatively, they will not usually be obvious. But the effect will be obvious: the viewer will feel himself involved in the film, with strong feelings about the different characters. The expressive power of these two uses of the camera is enormous.

AMAZING SPIDER-MAN is published by NON-PAREIL PUBLISHING CORP. OFFICE OF PUBLICATION: 625 MADISON AVENUE, NEW YORK, N. Y. 10022. SECOND CLASS MAIL PRIVILEGES AUTHORIZED AT NEW YORK, N. Y. ADDITIONAL ENTRY AT Meriden, Conn. Published monthly except November, semi-monthly. Copyright ©1966 by Non-Pareil Publishing Corp., all rights reserved, 625 Madison Avenue, New York, N. Y. 10022. Vol. 1, No. 43, December, 1966 issue. Price 12¢ per copy. Subscription rate $1.75 and $2.25 Canada for 12 issues including postage. Foreign subscriptions $3.25 in American funds. Prices do not include King Size Special November Issue. No similarity between any of the names, characters, persons and/or institutions in this magazine with those of any living or dead person or institution is intended, and any such similarity which may exist is purely coincidental. Printed in the U.S.A. by The Eastern Color Printing Co., Waterbury 20, Conn. Martin Goodman, Publisher.

56

DON'T GO 'WAY, FRANTIC ONE! ORIGIN TIME IS COMIN' UP--!

IF NOT FOR THAT BLASTED WALL-CRAWLER, I'D HAVE CAPTURED COLONEL JAMESON BY NOW!*

MY PLAN WAS PERFECT --FOOLPROOF-- TILL HE BUTTED IN!

*AS PROUDLY PORTRAYED IN OUR LILTIN' 41ST ISH! YOUR FRIENDLY FOOTNOTER--STAN!

BUT, I'LL FINISH SPIDER-MAN OFF! I'VE GOT THE POWER TO DO IT--THE POWER THAT THEY GAVE ME! I STILL REMEMBER HOW IT FIRST STARTED--

I WAS A NOBODY --JUST A HIRED HOOD--A MUSCLE-MAN, DOIN' THE DIRTY JOBS FOR A BUNCH OF PROFESSIONAL SPIES--

REMEMBER--WE OWE ALLEGIANCE TO NO NATION-- EXCEPT THE COUNTRY THAT PAYS US THE BEST!

AND YOUR ALLEGIANCE IS ONLY TO US!

SURE-- SURE!

MY ASSOCIATES THINK YOU ARE TOO STUPID TO BE TRUSTED--BUT I DISAGREE!

I FEEL YOUR VERY LACK OF INTELLIGENCE WILL PREVENT YOU FROM EVER BETRAYING US!

I DON'T CARE WHAT I DO-- SO LONG AS I GET PAID!

THE EXPERIMENT! TELL HIM OF THE EXPERIMENT!

AH, YES! WE SHALL GIVE YOU A CHANCE TO BECOME IMPORTANT--TO BE FAMOUS!

EXCELLENT! THAT IS WHY YOU ARE SO USEFUL TO US!

"THE EXPERIMENT TOOK MONTHS! MONTHS OF INJECTIONS--TREATMENTS--USING ME AS A GUINEA PIG, UNTIL--FINALLY--"

NOW FOR THE MOST CRUCIAL PART! YOU MUST LIE MOTIONLESS-- DO NOT MOVE A MUSCLE!

WE ARE ABOUT TO APPLY MY GREATEST INVENTION--

A FORM OF MOLECULAR ADHESIVE, WHICH WILL BECOME AS MUCH A PART OF YOU AS A SECOND SKIN!

THERE! IT IS DONE! OUR TREATMENTS HAVE GIVEN YOU THE STRENGTH OF A RHINOCEROS!

AND, THE MOLECULAR ADHESIVE COVERING YOU WEAR WILL GIVE YOU A PROTECTIVE SKIN TOUGHER THAN A RHINO'S OWN!

YOU ARE POSSIBLY THE STRONGEST MAN ALIVE--THANKS TO US! YOU MUST OBEY OUR EVERY COMMAND!

YOU WILL BE THE PERFECT ASSASSIN! BRAINLESS--OBEDIENT-- INVINCIBLE!

"BUT, THEY HAD MADE ONE FATAL MISTAKE! WHEN MY POWER INCREASED--MY INTELLIGENCE DID, ALSO!"

WHY SHOULD I SERVE YOU?

BAM!

I'M TOO STRONG TO TAKE ORDERS FROM ANY MAN!

5

71

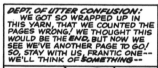

3: ARRANGEMENT

A scene from the National Film Board of Canada production CORRAL

Film has the unlimited capacity of making us notice things—simply by focusing on them or by centering everything around them. The arrangement of people and objects on the screen is important for directing our attention, and for suggesting the meaning of what is happening on the screen. Here again, comic books can be illuminating. In the *Spiderman* comic, you can tell about the action (and even the situation) simply from the arrangement of characters and objects.

There are no limits to the various ways in which people and objects can be arranged creatively in a shot. Everything depends on the situation, the characters, the basic action the shot describes. Generally, though, the difference between imaginative, expressive arrangement and a dead, static arrangement will be obvious. One communicates; the other does not.

bannisters and doorways are used to create that twilight feeling of an intermingling of light and darkness. THE PAWNBROKER, a powerful film about a man incapable of coming to grips with his tormented, haunting past, suggests a divided man by frequently throwing sharp light on one side of his face and leaving the other side dark.

Again, there are no rigid rules about the use of lighting: simply the general demand that lighting be used for more than realism—that it be highly expressive of what the film maker is trying to communicate. A film like END OF SUMMER, which attempts, wherever possible, to use natural lighting, does not fail at the same time to be most expressive—for the natural, realistic lighting gives a vivid sense of the immediacy and warmth of the scenes.

4: LIGHTING

Most amateur photographers, stepping out for the first time with a Brownie camera or even an 8mm. camera, think of lighting as a necessary evil —a problem they have to get around if they want to get a clear picture. Unfortunately, many professional film makers have fundamentally the same attitude toward lighting. But lighting can be expressive in a film: it can speak as strongly as camera angle, camera distance, or arrangement. It can heighten suspense, can lighten the mood, can provide an external reflection of the feelings of the characters.

In the sensitive French film CHILDREN ADRIFT, the story is told almost entirely by changes in lighting. The film opens at dawn. A French boy, made an orphan by the war, lives in a refugee camp. He awakens, washes, and eats his small breakfast. His morning is buoyant: he does things like chasing a train and rolling down a dusty hill on cardboard with other boys. All this time the sun is shining,

although more and more dimly. By afternoon he is sadder, quieter; and the sun has gone behind a cloud. Late in the afternoon — now with clouds darkening the sky — he finds his uncle, the man who has taken care of him, pushing a cart of rags. Suddenly the old man collapses; with the help of his companions, the boy pushes the man's body to the hospital in town. By the time they have reached town, it has rained; when the boys emerge from the hospital, the streets are almost dark, with whatever light there is reflecting from the wet sidewalks. The sadness of the scene reflects the boy's grief at his loss and the seeming indifference of the other boys.

Few films attempt to use light so significantly as CHILDREN ADRIFT. But many films use light expressively: to interpret character, to bring out the full drama of a scene, or to increase a sense of mystery by the use of shadows. In suspense films like HUSH ... HUSH SWEET CHARLOTTE shadows of

Before color was technically possible in films, many people thought that black and white was a terrible drawback for a film—and that once color became possible, no one would ever make a film in black and white again.

FIVE: COLOR

Strangely enough, films are still being made in black and white. And not always because the budgets weren't large enough for color. Peter Ustinov, who made the film BILLY BUDD, refused to make it in color. "Color beautifies everything," he said, "and I never feel you get the conditions of people in color." Indeed, black and white contains a number of expressive elements that color film cannot use. A color film cannot use shadows very effectively—the amount of light needed to shoot a film

A scene from the National Film Board of Canada production PHOEBE

in color obliterates most shadows. A grim, earnest movie loses some of its seriousness in color. The tone of a film can be controlled better when the director is dealing in black and white; very few color movies have been made in which the tone was highly controlled.

If color is to be used, it should be used above all with restraint. The first five years of colored films were an extravaganza of reds and oranges, yellows and blues: often unnecessary, sometimes blinding colors. No film has been perfected that captures colors as they are seen by the eye. The colors in films are always a little off and generally a little brighter than the colors we see in daily life. The danger should be obvious. Films made in color will

tend, simply by the fact, to glitter—as Ustinov said, "to beautify everything."

A good example of restraint is the feature animated film ANIMAL FARM. Based on the political satire by George Orwell, this film attempts to use color as a constructive, expressive element in the story. All the colors are diminutives of red: browns or pinks or oranges. There are no blues, no greens. The effect is a sharpened sense of the struggle for power that goes on in the barnyard, an increase in the feelings of awe and outrage.

Of course, the color can be completely controlled in an animated cartoon; it cannot be in a regular feature film. Yet some recent film makers have shown that color can be controlled much more than was thought possible. Little things—a bystander's red dress, a moon seen through an orange filter, a dark blue carpet — can reflect personalities, can contribute to an overall tone that the film might be attempting to create. Color has never been a strongly expressive element in films, but that doesn't mean it can't be.

Films may be able to reproduce reality and make life seem to come alive again on the screen. But when the people making the film are alert and wish to communicate, a film can do more than duplicate visual reality. It can be highly expressive — can make potent statements about man, his condition, his failures and successes. It is only when a film reaches beyond the effort to reproduce life and uses its language to express something creatively that it is capable of becoming an engaging and uplifting experience.

A scene from the National Film Board of Canada production YOU'RE NO GOOD

THE LANGUAGE OF MOTION

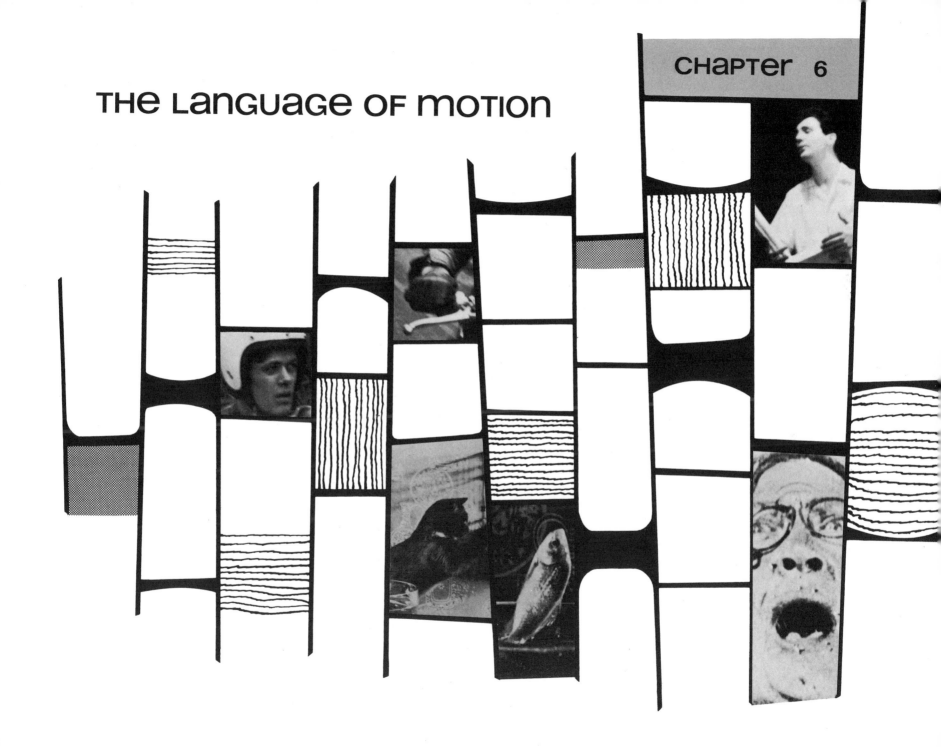

The picture may be an important part of the language through which film speaks. But even more important—and more fundamental to the film—is movement.

Movement, as we said, is the essence of a motion picture. Lively, effective films have been made in which there is no picture—only abstract designs merging into one another. But no film has been made—with any success, at least—in which there is no motion. Even if the motion is only the drifting glitter of sunlight on a lake, or a buzzing fly, or the mumbling lips of a dying man, these can arrest the viewer's attention and keep the movie moving.

We said about the picture that its first and foremost effort should not be to reproduce life: rather, to express. Can the same be said of movement? Movement seems to be so much a part of life and so basic that it would not tend to be highly expressive. Yet movement can be expressive, and it can be highly revealing. And as with the language of the picture, much of the language of movement can be missed unless the viewer is highly attentive.

A film can move in four different ways. The most fundamental form of movement is the movement of the subject: generally the actors. The expressiveness of gestures, a suddenly outthrust fist, a slow, grave walk are forms of the language of motion. A car spinning out of control, a tree crashing to the ground, a gun thrown into the ocean: these motions can be highly expressive, though the motions are not actually those of people moving.

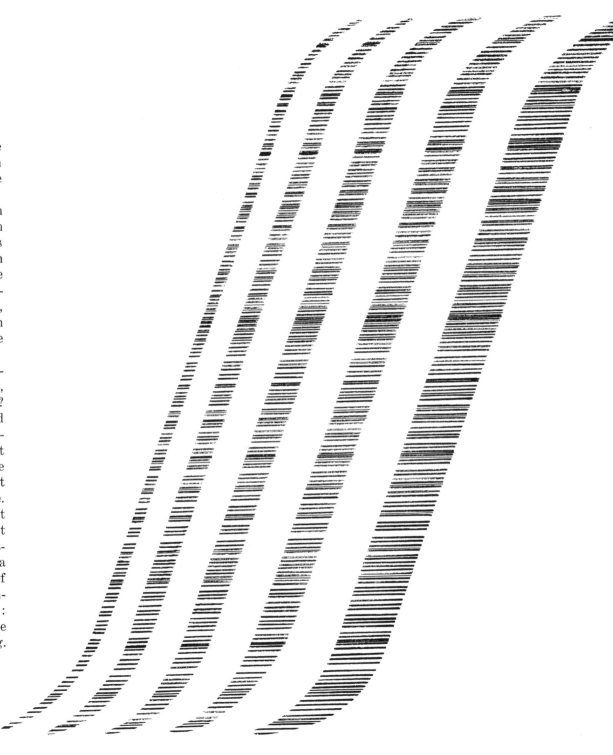

at matters in the motion of subjects on the een is not simply that people and things move that the movement itself brings about a greater vement, a progression within the film.

The second kind of movement is closely related the first: the movement of background. In the gnant British film A TASTE OF HONEY, the story set against a major industrial river of London. e constant motion of barges on the river and ving smoke from the background factories give film a sense that life is all part of a great in- strial jungle. Background movement, while not erally as expressive as the movement of the ors, can contribute greatly to the mood and the rall effect of a film.

These two forms of movement—of the central ion and of the background — are fundamen- and generally very obvious. The film cannot vive without them. But the film can move in other ways: through camera movement and ting.

Camera movement can be an important source novement, and a richly expressive aspect of film guage. Suppose a man is playing a game of ds, not simply for money but betting for his He has been caught cheating at cards by angster king, brought to the gangster's head- rters, and now must honestly defeat the man plus two of his own cardsharps. The drama is taut —but how is the camera to record it? Certainly fast editing, flashing back and forth from the dif- ferent faces, can be effective. But another way would also be the clever use of camera movement. The camera could track (move on a wagon) around the table, glimpsing one face after another, always viewing the crucial center of the table. The camera could also focus on each individual and move up and down (the term is tilt) to show each face and pair of hands. In such a situation, the possibilities for expressive camera movement are rich.

Admittedly, the possibilities are not always rich, and effective camera movement generally demands a great deal of restraint. It is always a temptation to switch scenes by means of a long panning shot (in which the camera moves horizontally right or left); but our eyes rarely move in this fashion, and an overuse of panning will seem contrived. Generally, camera movement is most effective when there is some drama generated between two or more characters or between a character and his situation—and only then when the characters do not themselves provide the movement.

It seems at this point that movement can't be so very expressive in the film after all. The pos- sibilities for actors, background, and camera move- ment are limited—so much so that motion does not seem to be a major expressive element in the language of film.

The best movies, however, are often those in which motion *is* the major expressive element; and if the motion does not come from the movement on the screen or camera movement, then it will prob- ably come from editing.

Editing—the joining together of two shots—is the only aspect of film that belongs exclusively to film and no other art. Painters, musicians, danc- ers, and writers can use many of the expressive elements of film: but no one else can use film edit- ing. Editing of moving sequences belongs exclu- sively to film. And editing is in many ways the central element in a film.

Imagine a sequence in which a man has escaped from a southern chain gang and is racing from the guards. They are chasing him with hounds, and he is racing toward a swamp. Suppose the camera were to follow the action — but without editing. With one camera and one roll of film, we could show only the man and not his pursuers (ex- cept from a very great distance). Then what we would see of the man would be continuous: we would see him running, running, running. Once he is in the swamp, the camera could pan the bog- gy surroundings and perhaps even catch a glimpse of an alligator or a water moccasin. But there would be almost no close-ups; the camera would be too busy keeping up with the man. What we would see, finally, would be a man racing and the surroundings he is racing into, with perhaps a glimpse of the men following him. The inherent drama of the chase would be almost completely lost.

Imagine, on the other hand, a creatively edited sequence in which the same man is racing from the guards. The sequence will lead up to a climax at which he grabs a vine and slips below the water as the guards and hounds pass only yards away. The opening shots would show his reckless running, his desperate facial expression; then the eager dangerous-looking hounds. Again the camera shows the man crashing through the undergrowth, with close-ups of his nervous, hurried hands pushing aside the brush, and his feet beginning to slap in the mud. Then perhaps a long shot of the dismal swamp, with close-ups of the treacherous mud, the lazy alligators, a water moccasin draped over a fallen tree. Again the dogs and the grim-faced guards; again the running man, panting now, up to his ankles in mud. Suddenly he stops and gasps: the cameras show the swamp as he sees it. He turns around. In the distant background the hounds pull several men forward. The fugitive lunges into the swamp. Close-ups of his shins, then his knees, then his thighs sinking into the muddy water. Again the hounds, their progress slowed by the water; the faces of the guards, satisfied that the fugitive is killing himself by entering the swamp. Next the camera shows the terrified man to his waist in water, almost incapable of motion. His face, suddenly in close-up, is stricken with terror. The camera cuts to a snake swimming just past his stomach. Again his face, gasping. A cut

to the guards at the edge of the swamp, trying to see the fugitive. Then the man, up to his shoulders in water, sees a loose vine. He grabs it and ducks beneath the water to avoid detection. The next shots show the guards as they patrol the firm ground around the swamp. The camera shows what they see: stretches of water, bayou trees, and hundreds of dangling vines. The searchers turn to leave, satisfied that the fugitive has run to his death.

There is really no difference in the story presented in this way — only in the means of telling it. But the effect of the difference is incalculable. Through editing — shooting from the fugitive to his pursuers back to the fugitive—the drama and suspense are charged with greater excitement, and the very story seems much more real. Yet what we are seeing in the second version is simply a collection of fragments, not really a whole story. The story now succeeds, however, because the fragments are key moments in the action, and we can fill in what they leave unsaid.

Editing is the life-force of a film. Much of the life can come to a film through the other forms of movement described earlier, but editing can mean —and usually does mean—the critical difference between a dead or living film.

It took a while for film makers to discover the importance of imaginative editing. The earliest film makers — notably the Frenchman Georges Melies with his trick photography, and the American director Edwin S. Porter—set their cameras in front of the action and let the film record things as they happened. Porter made a step toward editing by inserting previously shot film within a larger film, but he still considered the film a whole —not an assemblage of fragments.

David Wark Griffith, American film maker, discovered that only part of the action needed to be shown. For example, in the monumental film he made in 1915, THE BIRTH OF A NATION, he was depicting the assassination of President Lincoln. His cameras made no effort to show the whole action at one time: the film cut from the President sitting down—to the bodyguard outside the box—to the President taking his wife's hand—to the play—to John Wilkes Booth preparing for the assassination. By this means, Griffith was able to heighten the tension even as he depicted the story in a highly dramatic way.

In the kind of continuity developed by Griffith, the action is rarely carried over from one shot to the next. The viewer nevertheless remains highly aware of the total action, because he is constantly seeing key details that both explain what is happening and help the story progress. Griffith convinced film makers and film viewers that a scene in which one man shoots another man with an arrow can be more convincing with two shots (taken perhaps weeks apart and in different places) than with one shot showing the total action. Griffith also showed that if the pace of the cutting moved faster, the tension mounted, and this could make a climax much more powerful.

Griffith's discoveries have enriched the film since his day. The glaring contrast between the kind of films he created through an imaginative use of editing and those being made in his day proves that good film making is strongly dependent upon editing.

The other major figure in the development of editing was the Russian genius, Sergei Eisenstein. Eisenstein had been educated to be an architect, and his fascination with mathematics would influence the films he made. Eisenstein said that if two images in a film are put next to each other —say a weak-looking general and a strutting peacock—the final effect would be a third meaning, different from the two images — in this case, a caustic comment on the general. All of Eisenstein's early films are filled with the effort to evoke this third meaning. In one movie, OCTOBER, he de-

Scenes from POTEMKIN, directed by Sergei M. Eisenstein, 1925. Courtesy of Museum of Modern Art/Film Stills Archive

picts the weak leader, Kerensky, and interjects a statue of Napoleon Bonaparte — another caustic comment. In THE BATTLESHIP POTEMKIN, Eisenstein expresses outrage at the criminal persecution by the Czar's troops by showing three quick shots of the palace stone lions—one is lying down, almost asleep; the next is beginning to rise, as if alerted; the third is up and roaring. The quick succession of the three stone lions make it seem as if they were one lion, and had suddenly come alive.

More than anyone else in the history of film Eisenstein explored the potential of editing. H carefully experimented with the method of shor ening the shots in an edited sequence with prec sion so that each shot became slightly shorter tha the one before it—leading to a high pitch of ex citement. In a famous sequence from THE BAT TLESHIP POTEMKIN, he attempts to show the hor ror of Czarist troops slaughtering civilians wh sympathize with a Navy rebellion by heightenin

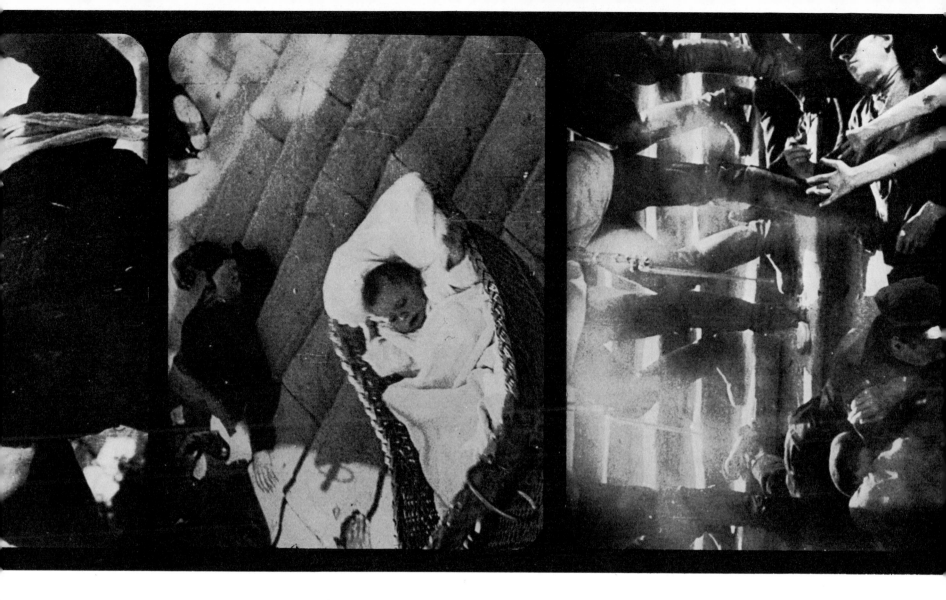

the tempo of his shots. The Czarist troops are shown approaching the Odessa steps, where crowds have been waving to the rebellious ship. Suddenly the gunfire starts; people scream, rush away. Bodies tumble, strewn over the steps. A baby carriage begins rolling precariously down the steps. A woman is shot in the face and screams. The baby carriage rolls on down the steps; no one stops it. The troops march insensitively down the steps, killing as they go. The pictures are potent enough, but the way they are put together, the way in which they move faster and faster across the screen, gives the whole sequence a powerful surge of horror.

The contributions of Griffith and Eisenstein were important: they opened the way to editing as a major expressive aspect of film language. Yet despite the existence of many well-edited films, movie makers continue to edit films only with the notion of preserving continuity. Continuity is essential (and several things will be said about it in the final chapter), but if editing is done with the sole idea of keeping the story together, the editing has little chance of being really expressive. And the film will suffer—noticeably.

How exactly can editing be expressive in a film? Griffith's use of dramatic editing is one way. Eisenstein's combination of two images to provide a third meaning is another. But editing can be used in still another way, and here be highly effective: in controlling time.

Griffith discovered that editing, in a sense, is time control—a way of slowing down or speeding up actual time. Most film makers use editing to speed up time. If a man is approaching his house, good editing can eliminate the need to show him making the whole walk: we could see him approach the house, then watch his back disappear behind the front door. Some film makers, however, have used editing to expand time: in a bridge-building sequence from one of Eisenstein's films, the action is viewed from several different camera angles and takes much longer than it does in real life.

But the really expressive potential in editing as time control is achieved when editing is used as a means of roving freely in the past, present, and future.

In the film YOU'RE NO GOOD, a boy named Eddie wants to steal a motorcycle. He stands across the street looking at the cycle and imagines an attempt to take it erupting into a struggle with two men who try to stop him. The thought is immediately overcome by another: the freedom he would have on a motorcycle. Finally, he thinks of taking his girl on a long ride, and that thought is decisive —he steals the motorcycle. Throughout the film, present, past, and Eddie's imagined future mix within a visual swirl that is actually the confusion of Eddie's mind. Often the conjunction of shots serves to confuse the story (which really is not that important), but gives the viewer a potent sense of Eddie's predicament, his antagonism toward authority (which is important). The film is a powerful and provocative experience: but the crux of the experience is not Eddie's acting, nor even his plight—but the way in which editing reveals his situation.

Scenes from the National Film Board of Canada production YOU'RE NO GOOD

In THE GOLDEN FISH, a boy brings home a magnificent goldfish, that he leaves in a bowl of water which is too small for the energetic fish. The fish and a canary get along quite well until a cat appears. The cat is dark, silent, and stealthy. He peers into the goldfish bowl, then plays with the canary, trying to get at either one. Careful shooting and careful editing tell the story most effectively: so effectively, in fact, that the viewer hardly notices the pace and tempo of the editing as the story progresses. When the goldfish, swimming frantically around and up and down in its bowl, eventually overshoots the bowl and begins flopping on the table, the cat — strangely enough — comes to its rescue.

Scenes from a Columbia Pictures release, THE GOLDEN FISH, a J. R. Cousteau production. Courtesy of Contemporary Films Inc.

89

Editing, despite tremendous power to express concepts and feelings, is generally inconspicuous. Good editing does not usually call attention to itself: it enables the full experience to come through. The same is true of any of the forms of the language of motion. These forms are attempting to communicate visually; and they are effective because of what they communicate—not because they are handled cleverly or stand out in the film.

Motion will always remain the heart of a good film, and the language of motion will remain central to the film's process of communication. A film that is highly expressive pictorially—with excellent lighting, fine camera angles, brilliant arrangement—but which doesn't move will probably be a dull movie, something like an art museum on film. The language that people crave, the language commercials have used so well, is a language of movement. Here movies communicate as nothing else can; here they find a form of expression that is wholly their own. It is a language worth getting to know.

a Language of sound

Imagine a movie describing the deprived people living in a stricken inner-city district. The camera explores their tattered, deteriorating apartments; we see the wallpaper shredding from the walls, the floors gaping with holes, the people sitting on orange crates or newspapers. As the camera reveals the dingy surroundings, the narrator comments: "These people live in poverty. Their homes are apartments that they pay too much for, and which no landlord keeps up. The walls are crumbling. The floors are filled with holes. The bathroom facilities often do not work. The people live with little furniture—and what they have is in terrible condition . . ."

The commentator's voice goes on, but at the expense of the film. Why? What has happened? It is the most frequent sin committed by makers of documentary and instructional films: too much talk.

Commentary can be most helpful in a film, but it can also be most *un*helpful. A good film, well photographed and imaginatively edited, can be ruined by an abundance of commentary. More than ruined: the final film will most likely be an outright insult to its audience. The commentator will continually be interrupting the viewer's experience and *telling* him what he is already seeing for himself. "The walls are crumbling." They certainly are. But the cameras say it better and more effectively than the commentator. Why does he have to bother trying?

Unfortunately, movies are still being made—especially for television—in which the eyes of the viewer are not respected, and the commentator must state verbally what the attentive viewer can grasp visually. The fact that these movies are so disastrously frequent raises the question of whether people *can* see for themselves when watching a film. And it raises the question of whether the film makers know what the role of sound should be in a movie.

There are basically four kinds of sound in films: natural dialogue (when actors speak), commentary, music, and sound effects. All of these forms of sound can contribute to the total language of film—or (and this is the most frequent use) they can distract from it. Indeed, the temptation with sound is to use it *to* distract—to make sure the message gets across to the viewer no matter what. And how best to make sure of this than to *state* the message—whether through a narrator, the pitch of violins as lovers kiss, or the unneeded statement by an actor, "I feel sick," when his face could have expressed the same thing?

The history of sound in movies is a brutal lesson in the danger of overusing sound. For 30 years (between 1897—the first movies—and 1927—the first sound movies) films were without sound. The words "spoken" by actors would be printed on "title shots" inserted between the regular shots. If the tall Texan wanted to tell the heroine that he must move on, the screen would suddenly show the words, "I'm sorry, Belle, but duty calls." This method was somewhat disturbing, but audiences became used to it. The great advantage was that movie makers had to find visual ways of expressing themselves and get along as best they could without the title shots. Consequently, some of the best films of the silent period (for example, Chaplin's films) use few or no titles — yet are thoroughly understandable.

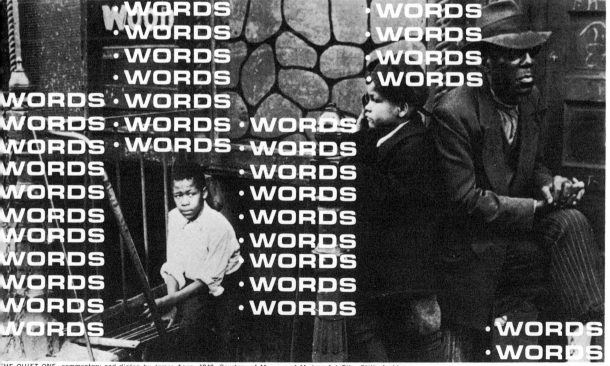

THE QUIET ONE, commentary and dialog by James Agee, 1948. Courtesy of Museum of Modern Art/Film Stills Archive

THE JAZZ SINGER, with Al Jolson.
Courtesy of Museum of Modern Art/Film Stills Archive

.... then sound came almost overnight

When sound came, however, with the Warner Brothers' film THE JAZZ SINGER, almost overnight the silent film disappeared. People wanted sound with their films—it was so much more natural. But the films made in the period following THE JAZZ SINGER were films that forgot many of the things discovered during the silent age. Suddenly the pictures became much more static. Actors didn't move around but stood around and talked. Most movies were more like Broadway plays than silent films. Comedies suffered; the wild, erratic slapstick of the Keystone Cops, Harold Lloyd, and Charlie Chaplin gave way to the punch-line humor of Bob Hope, Jack Benny, and the Marx Brothers. Sound didn't just add to films; it infected them, stifling so many of the other methods of expression that had been learned.

It took a while for film makers and audiences to realize that a sound-infected film was not necessarily a more fascinating film than one in which sound was used sparingly. Indeed, the good directors came to recognize that movies which were too "talky" were visually dead; and directors like John Huston and Alfred Hitchcock began to move away from the heavy emphasis on sound and depict their situations through almost wholly visual means. The discovery by these directors — and eventually by many others—was a critically important one: sound in a film must fit within the total film language, and not attempt to be a language all its own.

The danger that sound would attempt to do all the work in a film is an understandable one. The rise of the sound film came right alongside the

THE KID, with Charlie Chaplin. Courtesy of Museum of Modern Art/Film Stills Archive

rise of radio, and radio was sometimes more influential in the creation of movies than it should have been. Also, a number of films were made from plays, and little care was taken to move the cameras or to edit imaginatively. More or less overlooked was the fact that movies come alive when they use the language that is theirs: a language of the picture, a language of motion—and, within this context, a language of sound.

How can sound be used expressively within a film? A number of films have succeeded in so using it. But how?

In 1965 an hour-long documentary, LET MY PEOPLE GO, was made for television by Wolper Productions. Visually, LET MY PEOPLE GO is a stirring and monumental tribute to the Jewish people of the twentieth century. It depicts their struggles to establish their own nation and the incredible sufferings and persecutions they underwent before they finally were able to make Israel their own country. The story is vigorously told through excellent clippings from newsreels, numerous facial shots, and well-paced editing. But the whole meaning of the film comes through only with the sound. The narrative is terse, but well-written; it states only what it must state. Often, when the shots are self-descriptive (such as some powerful scenes of Nazi persecution of the Jews), the narrator is silent. The music, however, really joins all the aspects of the film together. A number of musical themes, most derived from Jewish hymns, recur throughout the film. At times they are sung: for instance, in the pathetic scenes of the Warsaw Ghetto in which Jews are dying in the streets. At other times the themes are played instrumentally. But the excellent interweaving of musical themes throughout the film gives it an organic unity that could never be attained in a silent film—a unity most documentaries lack.

A film such as LET MY PEOPLE GO suggests that sound can be a tremendous advantage to an imaginative film maker—but only when used within the total structure of the film and not as the major form of expression. Sound must always be part of the total film language—never a language attempting to carry the load by itself.

As was mentioned earlier, there are four ways in which sound can be used in films: dialogue, commentary, music, and sound effects. Each kind of sound has its own method of expression and its own limitations.

Dialogue is the form of sound we are most familiar with and which we expect most naturally from movies. The silent films were supplied with music (most theaters had a house organist or piano player), and the commentary was never obtrusive

© 1960, Columbia Pictures Corp., ON THE WATERFRONT, an Elia Kazan Production with Marlon Brando. Courtesy of Film Center, Inc.

A Continental Distributing Inc. release, Jacque Tati's MY UNCLE

n the title shots. But to see a man's lips move and then wait a moment to read what he said—no wonder people anxiously waited for sound.

Dialogue is so integral a part of most acted films that it is difficult to distinguish between the visual communication and the dialogue. Generally though, heavy dialogue slows down the movement in a picture and puts the whole work of communication on the dialogue. Plays converted into films usually suffer from this defect. Even such a superb film as A MAN FOR ALL SEASONS (which deservedly won five Academy Awards) is marred by its great dependence upon dialogue.

A film that uses dialogue only when it has to—THE GUNS OF NAVARONE is a good example—and which uses gestures, action, facial expression as much as it can, will seem better made than the film that uses dialogue as a crutch. In the latter case, the actors say everything, even when much could have been stated through visual expression.

A problem here is that a number of films deal with situations which require heavy dialogue. Some recent Swedish psychological dramas, for example, depend on the words of the characters more critically than a chase-filled suspense thriller. There are no ironclad rules about the use of dialogue in film, only the need to keep the dialogue within the total language of film.

Commentary is basically a different kind of thing than dialogue. Dialogue emerges from the very nature of a fiction film: if there are actors, it is only natural that they speak. But a commentary, no matter how well handled, will always be something of an intrusion, an interruption into the basically visual communication of the shots. Admittedly, commentary is an absolutely necessary intrusion: generally we would not understand what the film is saying without it. But the danger

that commentary will be overbearing is even more pronounced than it is with dialogue. We are so used to getting our information through words that the script writer of a documentary, even if he is a weathered professional, will tend to say more than he needs to say. Consequently, there are relatively few films with commentary in which the expression is mainly visual and not narrated.

Some of the best examples of films in which commentary is kept to a minimum are well-made commercials. A recent series of malt liquor commercials might have been absurd, but they communicated visually with only a touch of commentary. A man dropped from a plane in a parachute with a tray of malt liquor, landed on a prepared sheet marked with a bull's-eye, served the waiting customer—and the only commentary was, "In the dull and commonplace occurrences of day-to-day living one thing stands out as a completely unique experience — Colt .45 malt liquor." Ridiculous? Yes, but effective. And that is what film language is all about — being effective.

© 1965, United Artists, TOM JONES, directed by Tony Richardson

so, who needs words?

Music, like commentary, is a special problem in films. Here again the tendency to overdo the use of music is powerful. Anyone who has seen some love scenes from movies of the early 1930's can remember the loud swelling of violins that would accompany every kiss. Music has been used with more restraint in recent years, but often films are made in which silence would be more effective at times than the music. If music is used too much, it will lose its appeal—like too much color or too much wine. Often music is best used (Hitchcock is good at this) when it leads up *to* a period of silence.

There are numerous ways in which music can be effectively integrated with the film. Most movies that have music composed for the film will have two or three themes running through the film which correspond to different people or key experiences. "Lara's Theme" from DOCTOR ZHIVAGO is a well-known example: the theme is heard the first time we meet Lara, and is repeated with the appearance of (or Zhivago's thoughts about) Lara throughout the film. Sometimes two themes will merge at the climax of a film, suggesting the merging of separate or conflicting elements.

Some recent films have used music in fresh, highly expressive ways. In the film THE LONELINESS OF THE LONG DISTANCE RUNNER, the director Tony Richardson uses jazz with shots of the young man running at dawn. The jazz conveys a sense of freedom. In the same film, Richardson makes a brutal comment by depicting the guards beating one of the boys who tried to escape from the reform school, with the background music being the other boys singing, "Jerusalem," a song of stirring hope. Music, as Richardson and others have shown, need not always reflect the spirit of what is happening: it can comment on the visual expression by contrasting with it.

Besides dialogue, commentary, and music there is another area of sound—what is sometimes called, slightingly, "sound effects." The importance for films of footsteps on stairs, a can clinking in an alley, the steady tapping of rain, can hardly be exaggerated. The use of natural sounds in a film can be a highly expressive element as well as a major source of dramatic effect.

In the film AN OCCURRENCE AT OWL CREEK BRIDGE, a Confederate civilian has been caught behind Union lines. He is to be hanged at dawn. The first five minutes of the film show the bridge, the terrified man, and the Union soldiers. But the real communication is in the sounds: we hear the reverberation of footsteps on the bridge, the twittering of awakened birds, the rush of water below as the man hears them—and they all herald his coming death. Then the man drops; but the rope breaks, and he lunges through the water to freedom. Again sounds are used in a most creative way. The splashing of water, the sound of birds and wind, now bring a sense of joy in being alive. Natural sounds become highly expressive elements in the total film.

Scenes from Films du Centaure-Filmartic production, AN OCCURRENCE AT OWL CREEK BRIDGE. Courtesy of Contemporary Films, Inc.

100

Some films, such as the short RUN!, use sounds not to mirror real sound but to catch the mind of a character. In RUN! a man is racing through deserted city streets from a pursuer in black. All we hear are the jumbled sounds in his frenzied mind: the mixture of cars, phonographs, all the sounds of the city jammed together. The effect is a strong sense of identification with the man.

Natural sounds can be used simply as that—natural sounds, a means of making the movie seem more realistic. But they can add to the suspense, the strength, the beauty of a movie if they are used with sensitivity and care. Here restraint is not so important as the simple effort to *be* expressive with sounds—an effort expended by relatively few film makers.

These four forms of sound in a film—dialogue, commentary, music, and sound effects—may seem to comprise the total language that we hear in a film. But there is another way in which to use the sound track expressively: through silence.

Silence can be more than the simple absence of sound. It can carry meanings and charge feelings more potently than any forms of sound can. In ordinary life, we know things are quiet when we can hear a slight noise or a noise coming from far away: the buzz of a fly or the passing of a train at a great distance. In a film, silence can sharpen our attention and encourage us to concentrate on the picture. A silent, grim face; a wordless moment when men drop their weapons—these can be extremely effective. Silence frees the viewer and enables him to experience a moment in a film without his feelings being guided by a musical theme or an actor's line.

Before the first sound film was made, Sergei Eisenstein, the great Russian film maker, said that the worst thing that could happen to film would be a total synchronization of visual image and the sound of that image—in other words, using sound purely for realistic effects. Other critics have made similar comments: sound tends, by its very nature, to be destructive of film language.

There is truth in Eisenstein's statement, if only partial truth. Sound, like any other element of filmic language, should strive for more than realism; it should strive to be highly *expressive*. But there is another reason why the statement is true. The early American film maker D. W. Griffith described what he was trying to do in making films when he said, "I want above all to make you *see*." Of course, a similar thing could be said of the role of sound in films. The film maker sensitive to the use of sound could well say, "I want above all to make you *hear*."

We hear badly. Our ears are so bombarded by everyday noises — traffic, radios, the noises of kitchens and factories and offices—that we come to hear, really hear, very little of what hits our eardrums. Sounds that we might find beautiful or fascinating or meaningful go unheard: even such obvious sounds as a telephone ringing or someone calling our name. But more than going unheard, many of the sounds around us exist only in a formless, confused kind of din; we cannot distinguish sounds or listen to a specific sound.

The film has within it the power to educate our ears. It can enable us to hear, just as it enables us to see, by its sensitive, precise use of sounds — words, music, or natural sounds. A song, the crash of a running hound through the underbrush, a stone falling to the ground: simple sounds as these can be significant and meaningful, as they almost never are in real life. And music—heard so often without really being heard — can become more beautiful, more meaningful than ever before — simply by its relationship to the visual language of the film.

It is when sound in film enables us to *hear better* that it is being used within the total scope of filmic language. For here we can be sure that the film maker is working with real sensitivity, and that he is attempting genuinely to integrate the sound within the total film experience.

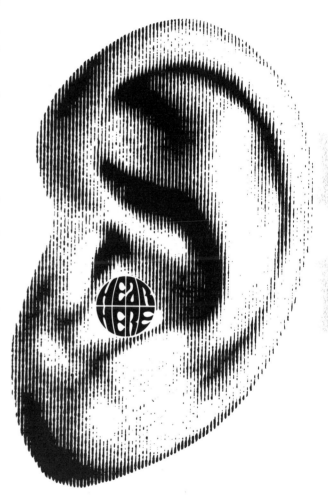

101

The last three chapters may seem to suggest that film language is really three languages: visual, moving, and audible. Actually, the language of film is a single language—just as English is a single language. The elements have been split up here to facilitate better understanding, but this division should not imply that the final film language is really a compendium of three languages. A movie is a movie; it speaks to us because it moves, because within it there are story, characters, and conflict which come alive before us. We understand the story, the characters, and the conflict because the film is able to communicate to us —and the way in which it communicates can be termed film language.

VISUAL MOVING AUDIBLE LANGUAGE = FILM

This introduction to film language has attempted to develop some of the basic ways in which a movie can be expressive. There are many other ways in which films can be expressive; film is a form of art which is highly alive and always searching out new forms of expression, new aspects of film language.

The rest of the text will deal with other various aspects of movies—their relation to drama, to the novel, how they can be made, etc. Fundamental to the coming chapters, though, will be our understanding that film is a language. Once some of the fundamentals of that language are understood, more will be taken from good films and less from poor ones.

non-PEOPLE CHARACTERS and PEOPLE CHARACTERS

CHAPTER 8

NON-PEOPLE CHARACTERS

There is a movie, made only a few years ago, about a decaying, haunted house and a girl pursued by the ghosts of the house. The girl, Eleanor, came to the house after caring for her mother for some 12 years; before she got there, she discovered that she and two others were part of an experiment to search out the ghosts of Hill House. A professor of anthropology, especially interested in psychic phenomena, was running the experiment, and he kept a careful account of all the incidents. The hauntings began the first night: loud footsteps in the hall, poundings on the door, and the twisting of the doorknob. Over the next few days, as the hauntings continued, Eleanor discovered that the ghosts of the house were after *her*. A lonely, frightened girl, Eleanor at first clung to the professor for security; but when the professor's wife suddenly appeared, Eleanor felt that the house needed her more than anyone else wanted her. One evening, as the hauntings reached a high, terrifying pitch, she ran wildly through the house to give herself to the ghosts. Eleanor was finally coaxed from a balcony (where earlier a servant had hung herself) and was to leave Hill House. Now, however, she wanted to be completely united with the house and never leave it. Driving toward the gate, she lost control of the car—someone else, someone unseen, was also at the wheel—and in dying, she became united with the house forever.

The credits in THE HAUNTING announce Julie Harris, Claire Bloom, and Richard Johnson as the main actors. Haven't they missed someone? In a sense: for anyone seeing the movie becomes quickly aware that the main character is not the professor, not even Eleanor; it is the house. Hill House has a personality all its own, and it dominates the film similar to the way in which Gregory Peck dominates a movie like TO KILL A MOCKINGBIRD. Early in the film we see the house for the first time, in the late afternoon sun: its enormous size, its strange, rising towers, its ugly walls all convey a mood of mystery. Within, we discover that no door is even but that all have been built at strange angles; an atmosphere of gloom and horror fills the great house. But we discover the house's true character at night. Robert Wise, who directed the film, began every evening in the film with impressive shots of the house's exterior: long-angle shots looking straight up at the towers or at the leering gargoyles jutting from the framework. Throughout the film there are over a hundred silent shots of the house, each one from a strong, unusual angle, each one suggesting the strange, disturbed nature of the old mansion.

Hill House in THE HAUNTING serves as an excellent example of the role that a "non-people character" can play in a film. The movies, because they can depict thoroughly not only people but the places and things that surround people, are probably the best medium for bringing out the "character" of a house, a forest, or an airplane. Anyone who has seen LAWRENCE OF ARABIA recalls how the long, shining desert seems to have been as important as Lawrence throughout the film. Or the road in LA STRADA: as the girl and her brutish companion travel from town to town, the road is their constant companion, their guide, their life.

Admittedly, not all films emphasize the role of places and objects to the point where they could really be considered "characters." But many films do; and the way in which these films develop their "non-people characters" is well worth looking at.

© 1963, by Metro-Goldwyn-Mayer Inc. and Argyle Enterprises Inc.: scenes from THE HAUNTING

A non-people character cannot be developed ·he same way a human character is developed. In ·TIZEN KANE, the character of Charles Foster ·ane is revealed in a dozen ways: through recol-·ctions of his friends; through glimpses of key ·oments in his life; through the man's way of ·cting — his cocksure speech, his domination of ·her people. But his immense mansion, Xanadu, ·ust be revealed in other ways. Quiet tracking ·nots down its endless halls, long shots revealing ·ne vast expanse of a single room, shot after shot ·f the immobile statues that stand like guardians ·round the house: all these bring out the desola-·on, the monstrous, inhuman dimensions of this ·reat vault Charles Kane has sealed himself with-·. In other words, a non-person character is de-·eloped largely through the camera: through ·amera angles and shots taken at carefully con-·rolled distances.

Basically, non-people characters exist in two ·ifferent ways: as places and as things. A "place" ·naracter may be a man-made place, such as a ·ouse or an office building; or it may be a natural ·lace, such as a wooded setting. Alfred Hitchcock ·s one of the best directors for using places to cre-·e an atmosphere to charge his films with added ·nsion or humor. In NORTH BY NORTHWEST, for ·xample, he is dealing with the typical spy chase ·neme (where a man, mistaken for a spy, is being ·nased across the country by foreign agents *and* ·e American police); but to keep the film from ·ipping into the same style as most spy chase ·nrillers, Hitchcock sets up his places in a very ·reative way. The key murder that begins the ·nase after Roger Thornhill takes place in a well-·t lobby of the United Nations building at noon—

of all places for an international murder, the un-likeliest. Fleeing to Chicago, Thornhill makes an appointment to meet the man he has been mis-taken for—George Kaplan—on a deserted road in the middle of a flat landscape. Here, with level, treeless land as far as one can see in any direction, he is attacked by a plane. The contrast between this noonday assault and the typical back-alley at-tack at dark so frequent in spy films gives NORTH BY NORTHWEST its special tantalizing quality.

Usually a place serving as a non-people char-acter will not be developed for its own sake, as in THE HAUNTING. Hitchcock and other directors generally use places to contribute to the atmo-sphere and the total dramatic effect. The woods in NORTHWEST PASSAGE, the snowy forests in DOC-TOR ZHIVAGO, the industrial river landscape in A TASTE OF HONEY: all of these contribute to the whole effect of the movies, although they are not meant to have an importance of their own.

THE RED BALLOON, directed and produced by Albert Lamorisse. Courtesy of Film Center, In

The role of objects as non-people characters in movies is slightly different. Objects, like people can move around or be moved: they can be developed by means other than pure camera placement and movement. One of the most well-known object "stars" of a film is the balloon in the French short THE RED BALLOON. From the moment the balloon is found tied to a street light, it moves and acts in surprising, uncanny ways. It obediently follows the boy who rescued it; when there is danger, it rises beyond arm's reach. One time after passing a blue balloon, it slips out of the boy's hand to follow the other balloon. Another time it pesters a school official who locked the boy up in an isolated room. By the end of the film the balloon is loved as much as any character in the film; and its destruction by the wanton street boys is terribly sad—like watching the death agonies of a good friend.

Often objects in films provide a type of direct symbolism which is so visual and immediate that they are not recognized as symbols. In a Swedish film WINTER LIGHT, a lonely priest stands for a long time next to a naked light bulb. His naked conscience is silently, effectively reflected by the naked bulb. These visual symbols are especially effective because, unlike most literary symbols, they needn't be thought out. The experience of seeing the naked light bulb is enough. Sometimes these symbols may become complex and mean more than just one thing—as Eddie's caged pigeons in ON THE WATERFRONT. Usually, though, visual symbols reveal their meaning immediately; and even if the viewer is not consciously aware of the meaning, he is struck by it as part of his experience of the film.

PEOPLE

CHARACTERS

It mustn't be thought that film stars will always e like Hill House, settings or things. Generally ne film stars are people who get credit for it: the ctors. And even if the actors are not the true creators" of a film (in the way that writer, di- ector, and editor are), they certainly contribute a reat deal to the finished movie.

Of all the elements in the film, we are probably ost aware and least aware of the actors. We are ighly aware of the "who" starring in a film, and it sually makes a big difference whether it is Steve IcQueen or some name we've heard of before. et once in the theater, we forget that the actors re acting; the whole thing seems so real that we lentify Steve McQueen with the role he plays— nd forget that what we are seeing has been acted ut.

This is one of the crucial differences between creen acting and stage, or live dramatic, acting. n front of a stage, we are kept conscious that this lay is being *acted out*—if simply because we have ne stage there to remind us of it constantly. But film moves so quickly and seems so real that we rdinarily do forget acting is involved, even when ne acting is superlative, such as Paul Scofield's A MAN FOR ALL SEASONS.

Film acting never was, fortunately, too heavily ifluenced by the styles and notions of stage act- g. The main reason was that films had to make neir own way for almost 30 years when they were ithout sound. The long period of silent films was

A scene from the National Film Board of Canada production PHOEBE

© 1962, United Artists. Harold Hecht's BIRD MAN OF ALCATRAZ, with Burt Lancaster

a blessing in disguise, for it enabled films to explore the kind of acting that was best suited to this new medium. Charlie Chaplin, the sad little tramp who became so successful during this period, has shown what kind of acting works best in the film. Chaplin's acting was totally *visual*: he would tilt his head, or strut in his bowlegged style, or clasp his hands nervously in front of him. His facial expressions would vary from delight at a girl's smile to indignation at an offense to sheer terror in being chased by a brutish enemy. And even more recently, it is the control of visible expression that makes an actor's acting so convincing; Marlon Brando mumbles his words but looks very sincere; in A MAN FOR ALL SEASONS, Paul Scofield speaks more convincingly through a lifted eyebrow than through a long speech.

This is not to say that the way in which an actor speaks his words doesn't matter in films. The camera, however, can show a face at very close range, and an actor must not only *speak* convincingly, his gestures and expressions must convey his feelings too—much more so in the theater. Live theater acting is done mainly through speaking, and usually loud speaking; the actor must be *heard* by everyone in the theater, and if the script calls for a whisper, it will only be a seeming whisper. In the theater an actor really must overact; he must use wide gestures and exaggerate every overtone

of expression so the whole audience can catch it. But the camera in a movie can come inches away from an actor—it can catch the tear gathering in a girl's eye, or the slow loosening of muscles around a knife in a gang leader's hand. And these slight expressions can be just as powerful as brilliant lines spoken in the theater.

The camera's power of close-range vision communicates in a new and startling way. There is tremendous power in a face, a potential for expression of any emotion a man or woman feels: joy, fear, anguish, boredom, sympathy. Any really well-acted film will probably use a great many close-ups. When we see the face of a young man terrified at his first experience of a battlefield, we have no doubt that *this is how he feels*. Speaking later to his companions, he might claim that he wasn't frightened, that he enjoyed the thrill of shooting a machine gun at the enemy. But once we have seen his face, we know; that is the direct power of facial expression.

Faces on a screen often say more than the movie viewers recognize. For the art of speaking through overtones of facial expression is a very subtle art and requires a subtle recognition (it might be worthwhile to examine the faces in these pages and try to describe just what feelings, even what kind of thoughts, they are expressing). Of course, the context of a movie is a great advantage in helping us understand what the face is revealing; the widow's face at a funeral will usually be drawn and haggard from grief at her husband's death. But many recent films have left a great deal of expression out of the words of the script and have depended upon the face of actors and actresses to communicate.

Naturally, there is more to good acting in a film than facial expression: everything about the actor—his walk, his style of speaking, his gestures, his dress—must seem real, an organic part of him. A character who speaks swiftly, in quick jagged phrases, will most likely walk swiftly, think things out quickly, and act suddenly, if not brashly. Inconsistencies in character are much more obvious on the screen than in the theater.

There are really no "rules" by which acting can be judged in a film. Good acting is obvious enough; so is bad acting. There is a kind of "non-acting," however—a rigidity of facial expression, a great restraint in being expressive in any way —which is sometimes very effective but more often deadly in films. Buster Keaton has always been successful with this style. Generally, when it is used (and television uses it frequently), this restraint from expressing feelings leads to a suggestion that the character *has* no feelings. It is very difficult to tell whether James Bond is happy, glum, or even alive in some of the shots from his films. This "non-acting" is a good thing to be on the watch for; it can reveal a lot about the quality and depth of a film—or more probably, a film's lack of quality and depth.

"Non-people characters," and "people characters" should both be fun to watch—interesting, fascinating, demanding our whole attention. Boring people and boring places really don't help a film, unless the director wants to communicate a certain boredom. This is another, and perhaps the best, index to an effective use of characters (both kinds) in the movies: If they're not fascinating to watch, they're probably not Worth watching.

FILMIC Drama

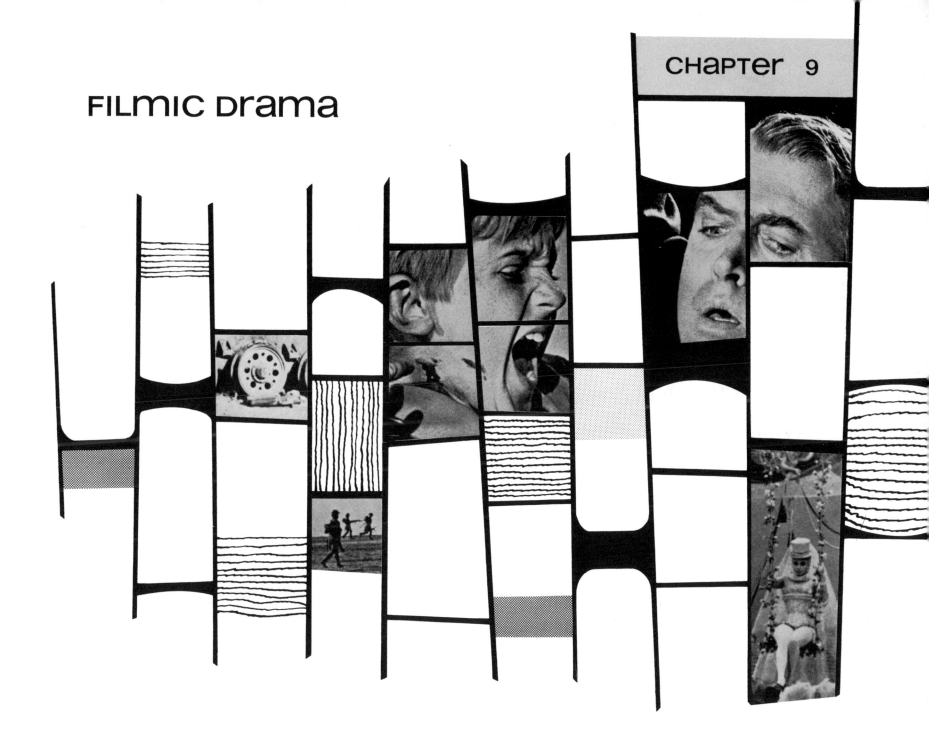

Scenes from VERTIGO, Alfred J. Hitchcock production, with James Stewart and Kim Novak. (© 1958, by Paramount Pictures Corp.)

VERTIGO was made by Alfred Hitchcock shortly before he made NORTH BY NORTHWEST. It is a strange, haunting film, and probably one of Hitchcock's finest. VERTIGO opens with Scottie, a police-detective, hanging by his fingers from the roof edge of a tall building. A policeman leans over to pull him up, but slips and falls to his doom. The experience gives Scottie vertigo, an abnormal fear of heights. It also shakes him up enough to quit his job on the police force.

He is eventually offered a new job by an old friend Elster, a shipbuilder. Madelaine, Elster's wife, lives in a trance; she seems to believe that she is another woman, Carlotta Valdes, who lived and died a century ago. Scottie is asked to follow and report on her. He accepts, and begins following Madelaine throughout San Francisco. But it is not San Francisco that Madelaine visits—rather, the tiny corners of the past tucked away in the city. She sits for half an hour daily in an art museum gazing at a portrait of Carlotta Valde; she stops in an old Spanish church, pauses before an unknown grave in a tiny cemetery. Madelaine exudes mystery, and soon Scottie finds that the fascination he feels for her is more than amazement at her fascination with the past.

Madelaine drives one day to the ocean and, after standing at the edge, plunges in. Scottie pulls her

t and takes her to his apartment; from this int on, he is as entranced as she. The two fall in ve—a love torn from within by Madelaine's pre-ccupation with the past. Then one dusk they visit e Mission of San Juan Baptista, where despite r promise of love, Madelaine rushes from Scot-e up the winding steps of the church tower. He ies to follow her but is overcome by the familiar rtigo. Shapes swarm; he spins dizzily, and sud-nly hears a scream, and out of the window sees e falling body of Madelaine.

Madelaine's suicide stuns Scottie, as it stuns the idience. After the inquest, we next see Scottie ring his slow, painful recuperation in a hospi-l. Even after he is out of the hospital, Scottie continues to yearn for Madeline, a yearning as acute and as mysterious as Madelaine's earlier yearning for the past. One day he sees a girl whose face resembles Madelaine; he follows her home, takes her to dinner, and eventually convinces her to dress as Madelaine, to color her hair and wear it like Madeline. As the resemblance in-creases we discover that the girl Judy actually was Madelaine—or was the girl who Scottie thought was Madelaine. She had stood that night with Madelaine's husband and screamed while he pushed another person to the roof below.

Scottie discovers that he had been duped, that the girl he loved was only a character in a macabre drama played out for him. Before admitting that he knows, he takes Judy back to the Mission. Gripping her arm tightly, he forces her up the steps. To kill her? To threaten her? At the top of the steps he reenacts for her what happened. The movie's conclusion contains Hitchcock's character-istic touch of final shock; it likewise reveals Scot-tie to be cured now of his vertigo and of his obses-sion with Madelaine, a kind of vertigo even more acute than his fear of high places.

Hitchcock's VERTIGO is, admittedly, a strange movie. The mood is haunting and merges reality with the unreal: death and the distant past. The major characters mystify and surprise us: Scottie, as well as we know him and identify with him, eventually proves to be a sick man. Madelaine is revealed to be an impersonation by a Kansas actress.

Yet VERTIGO is an excellent example of filmic drama—drama in which not only characters are involved, but also all the controlling forces in a movie: music, camera, lighting, editing, setting.

Drama is a major form of Western literature. Ever since the Greeks held their rituals to the fates, acted out in tragic dramas, men have attempted to express their feelings and aspirations through live action and speech. But drama has been, at least until this century, limited to the theater. Actors had to perform live before audiences in large houses or open places. Consequently, the expressive potential of drama was limited to speech and wide gestures. Any actor who had to communicate to a thousand or fifteen hundred people could not very well be expressive through slight changes in facial expression, nor could he use natural scenery—an oceanside, a desert, a mountainside. The audience always remained at a set distance from the actors. Within these limitations (and others), drama developed. Perhaps largely because of these limitations we have a heritage of Western drama especially rich and profound in its use of language.

Our understanding of drama, consequently, remains an understanding developed through theater drama. We therefore think of drama strictly in terms of the tensions and confrontations between individuals, expressed through language. A "highly dramatic" moment is one in which, for example, an actor lunges out in a roar of passion—as Shakespeare's King Lear in the storm. Language offered the major form of dramatic expression to the theater. It is only natural that we would think of drama in terms of language.

Film, however, uses much more than language: the expressiveness of a face gritted in pain, fingers of a hand tapping nervously on a desk, a car screeching around a deadly curve—these are not possible in theater. But does that mean they are not dramatic?

True drama reveals man—his struggles, his fears, his hopes. To see the young hero of BALLAD OF A SOLDIER lunge zigzag across a burnt-out battlefield when he is pursued by a tank involves no language; it is a moment impossible for the stage. But can we say this is not dramatic? As the boy struggles with a dead soldier's bazooka we can see hope flicker in his terrified face. The hope explodes into excitement and relief when the tank, almost upon him, stops dead from the bazooka shot. This is not dramatic?

Film has expanded the range of drama. It has taken drama beyond the stage, beyond the basic expression of language, and has given drama a new set of expressions. The world, which could be brought onto the stage only through language and the audience's imagination, now *can* be brought into drama. And the world—especially the highly complex world of today—is an inherent part of the real human drama that men live. GRAND PRIX does not show the Formula 1 cars roaring through the big races simply to get some exciting shots between the real dramatic action in the hotels and garages. The cars provide much of the drama; they are extensions of their drivers, and what the bold American's car does he is doing.

© 1963, Universal-International, Alfred J. Hitchcock's production THE BIRDS

In Hitchcock's film THE BIRDS, a small California town is faced with the terror of birds that swoop down to ravage and kill the people. There is drama (or more precisely, melodrama) in this film, but the birds play an important part. Not only are they a kind of collective "non-people character," but they are also an indispensable aspect of the film's drama. A drama impossible, of course, in a theater.

In the Russian film THE BATTLESHIP POTEMKIN, the point at which the Cossack soldiers (defenders of the Czar) come marching down the steps where hundreds of civilians are standing is horrifying. The horror is intensified by the increasing tempo of the scene changes, so that the violence seems to get worse and worse. Again, filmic and not verbal language is used: but this is drama, great drama.

VERTIGO, outlined early in the chapter, is a brilliant example of the use of full filmic drama. Filmic drama includes many of the dramatic elements possible in the theater: persons revealing themselves through their dialogue; a dependence upon intense, convincing acting; the growing involvement of the audience. Scottie, played by James Stewart, is a fascinating character with whom Hitchcock wants us to sympathize—indeed, this sympathy is fundamental to the film's effect.

Sympathy with a central character has been a characteristic feature of many theatrical plays; by controlling and perhaps abruptly shifting this sympathy, the playwright has always been able to secure his grip upon audiences. The confrontations in VERTIGO are likewise dramatic in the sense that they would be in a theater: Scottie's slow willingness to accept Elster's offer to follow his wife; Scottie's gradual involvement with Madelaine, culminating in his total isolation after her

seeming suicide; and eventually his rash, desperate efforts to make Judy impersonate Madelaine. VERTIGO uses language and depends for character revelation upon language.

Yet the drama in VERTIGO involves elements impossible on the stage. The film is suffused, for example, with a sense of place. We do not discover Madelaine through her speech (we wait a long time to hear her say anything); we discover her through the places she visits: the Carlotta Valdes portrait in the museum, the old Spanish church, the tiny graveyard. Whenever Scottie talks with her (except when they are in his apartment), it is in a place dominated by the past—among the Sequoias, at the edge of the ocean, in the Spanish mission. And key dramatic moments throughout the film (the opening shot, and the two times in the Spanish bell tower) reveal Scottie not through anything he *says*, but through his reaction to *where he is*—in a high place.

The drama in VERTIGO is also heightened by Hitchcock's highly controlled use of the camera. In a play the audience's sympathy with a character must be created through the character's lines. Hitchcock opens his film with a daring identification with Scottie by the use of subjective camera. We see Scottie hanging from the roof, then watch through his eyes as the policeman plummets to his death. Later we are in Scottie's car, behind the steering wheel, following Madelaine through San Francisco. The dramatic effect of identification with Scottie is achieved largely through such careful use of the camera.

Editing takes this identification with Scottie even further. In the second part of the film, while recuperating in the hospital, Scottie has a nightmare. Were VERTIGO a play, Scottie would have had to describe the nightmare for us to learn about it. Hitchcock shows us Scottie's nightmare; we experience it with him. Likewise, flashback shots of the original experience on the roof, and later of Madelaine, constantly build up our sympathy for

cottie. Moments of high dramatic tension, such s Scottie's first experience in the bell tower, are iven added dramatic impact by the fast editing.

It should be clear at this point that a movie like ΕRTIGO simply cannot be judged as a drama if ιe meaning of "drama" depends totally upon ctors and how well they speak their lines. The irector is more responsible for the dramatic efact of a movie than all the actors combined. In-deed, some films are able to achieve genuine dramatic effect with little or no help from actors. DESERT VICTORY, a World War II documentary depicting the Allied victory over Rommel's forces in North Africa, contains no actors; we hardly see any one person more than once. Yet the film is filled with real drama: a drama of tanks, guns, and planes—again, extensions of characters we know only as "Allies" or "Germans."

Stage drama has always centered on man. Whatever could be said about man through actors uttering lines was potential material for the stage. Film drama still centers around man. But it is as if man were now relocated—now placed within a world, a visual world, where we can see him, and see him in relation to his cities, his creations, his total historical setting. Stage drama used language. Film drama uses its own language: a language of visual images, of motion, and sound. Stage drama depended on actors. Film drama can use actors, or it can do without actors. Unlike stage drama, its characters can be people or the places and things with which people live.

The final effect of film drama, however, should not be so distant from the final effect of stage drama. We should be brought to understand man and his condition a little better. If a movie doesn't give us some understanding of man—if, on the contrary, it presents an unreal dream world—then it has failed as filmic drama.

Rizzali Film Distributors Inc. release, Federico Fellini's production, JULIET OF THE SPIRITS, with Guilietta Masina

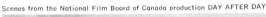
Scenes from the National Film Board of Canada production DAY AFTER DAY

THE FICTION FILM

FOUR HUNDRED BLOWS, directed by Francois Truffant. Courtesy of Museum of Modern Art/Film Stills Archive

So far we have mentioned that there are two basic kinds of films—the fiction film, made with actors and a prepared script, and the fact, or documentary, film, made directly from real-life events. Not much has been said about these two kinds of film, but the distinction cuts to the core of film, and understanding the distinction can promote a better understanding of movies. Many of the values of a movie (for example, expert acting or effective sets) stem from the kind of film it is: a fiction film or a fact film. And to become sensitive to these values, it helps to become sensitive to the basics of the fiction film and the documentary film.

To begin with, not all films are either fiction or documentary. Some, like IN COLD BLOOD, treat real-life events with a chilling, almost documentary realism. Then there are animated films, those documentaries that contain more fiction than fact (for example, the ones made by the Germans during the 1930's), and films that are a curious mixture of documentary and fiction-film technique— such as those made by the Russians during the 1920's. Nevertheless, most films can still be categorized as basically either fictional (with ev-

erything prepared beforehand) or documentary (which depends on things as they happen). Other types of films, such as experimental and instructional films, are not included because they are either using film language in new ways or, as with instructional films, not really using film language at all.

The fiction film generally tries to re-create some episode or story in life, to present life as it has been prepared by the writer, director, set designer, and actors. The key word is *preparation*. Most films are made by following a script that describes in detail each action: the camera's distance and angle, where the actors are located, what they say, how they say it, where they move—pretty much everything. A recent trend in movies (and some television shows) has been to permit the actors spontaneity—giving them only the situation and letting them handle everything from

there. NOBODY WAVED GOODBYE and French films like THE FOUR HUNDRED BLOWS are good examples of this technique. But most films continue to be made with a very detailed script.

When the team consisting of writer, director and actors put together a fiction film, they are not simply attempting to re-create life—they are attempting to make some kind of a statement about it. The statement may be that life is basically futile or funny; the statement of a typical bedroom comedy is generally that life contains nothing worthwhile besides sex. But every fiction film, no matter how badly or well made, makes some statement, some value judgment, about life For any attempt to re-create life involves a judgment that what is being re-created is *worth* all the trouble involved. Admittedly, many movies probably aren't worth all the trouble involved (and a good number of television shows certainly aren't)

124

but the point here is that the fiction film, by its very existence, makes a statement about life. And usually that statement can be recognized.

Take the film ON THE WATERFRONT, for instance. Here Terry Malloy, a young dock worker on the troubled Brooklyn waterfront, becomes involved in a conflict between the waterfront racketeers and a priest attempting to expose the whole set-up. The film is handled almost as a documentary: filmed on location, with strong shots of the waterfront area and strong, natural acting, ON THE WATERFRONT gives an instinctive sense of actually happening. The drama focuses around the character of Terry Malloy—a character who continues to emerge, almost as if from a cocoon, throughout the film. ON THE WATERFRONT is violent, but it presents life as having some order, justice, and hope. A much less brutal film, THE TROUBLE WITH ANGELS, may even touch upon a religious topic (little girls and nuns) but says much less hopeful things about life—that life is shallow, and for all its feeble moments of humor, is not really funny.

The fiction film, more than any other kind of film, must achieve an organic unity. Anyone familiar with biology knows that there is more unity in the organism of a cat than in a long string of algae. For the cat is much more complex: its body involves numerous functions and must work together as a whole. Algae are simply long strands of little one-celled organisms stuck next to one another. A feature fiction film is generally more complex than any other kind of film. The unity in a newsreel or a cartoon or even a lengthy documentary film is much like the unity of algae: simply repeating the same kinds of shots, keeping the same kind of dialogue, and binding the whole thing together with some story or idea. But the unity achieved in a good feature film is much more complex. Here the entire film is prepared in advance: the film makers can control cameras, settings, story, actors, action, sound—everything. And the final effect should be an organic unity—a unity much more complex and involved than that of other kinds of film.

© 1960, Columbia Pictures Corp., scenes from ON THE WATERFRONT. An Elia Kazan Production with Marlon Brando. Courtesy of Film Center, Inc.

HIGH NOON is the story of a marshal (Gary Cooper) who learns one morning that a man he has sent to prison is returning on the noon train to kill him. It is the marshal's wedding day, and he is encouraged by everyone to leave town. But the marshal knows his duty, and he knows that with the help of the townspeople he can stop Frank Miller and his gunmen. The town, however, refuses to help. The marshal cannot recruit anyone to stand up against the gunmen; and finally, when they enter town at noon, he must face them alone. He does, and courageously. With the help of his wife he is able to stop all of the killers. The conclusion of the film is the marshal's dropping of his badge in resignation.

Scenes from HIGH NOON, a Stanley Kramer Production. Courtesy of Museum of Modern Art/Film Stills Archive

But the story is only part of HIGH NOON: much more important are how the story is told and the questions it raises. Time is a vital factor in HIGH NOON. Clocks are shown frequently; the music continually reminds us of the coming train at noon. And the cowering, terrified reactions of the townspeople suggest that the real conflict of the film is not between the marshal and Frank Miller, but between the marshal and the people who refuse to back him up.

HIGH NOON achieves a quality of organic unity rare in a movie. There is nothing that could be taken out without having the film suffer. Each scene contributes to the total effect; each moment builds on the moment before. The tension is created from within the film—from the marshal's dilemma—rather than being imposed from outside. The characters are consistent: the stalwart courage of the marshal, the timid indifference of the townspeople, the love of the marshal's wife overpowering her abhorrence of violence. HIGH NOON achieves unity, but more importantly, it achieves an organic unity.

There are so many aspects to the fiction movie—character, plot, conflict—that it is difficult to speak in general terms about this kind of film. Beyond the two criteria mentioned above—a film's statement about life, and its organic unity—how distinguish a well-made fiction film from a crude one? Some rules of thumb might be to look for some depth in the treatment of a situation and some originality in the approach—and, of course, an effective use of filmic language. There is something, too, in a film's being basically believable: James Bond and a number of similar spies simply aren't believable; we know they could never happen. Science fiction films don't strain our powers of belief, but we aren't asked to believe in them to begin with. In the case of a fiction film, because it can come so close to being real, we are expected to believe the story. This being so, it should give us a story and characters that are capable of belief. The marshal in HIGH NOON is believable; so (and even more so) is Terry Malloy in ON THE WATERFRONT. Batman is not; James Bond is not. The difference is a big one.

Fiction films will probably continue to be the major form of film produced by the commercial studios and (in the form of series) produced for TV. Any growth in appreciation for these films will best come from a growth in taste, a development of sensitivity—values that can't be gotten from a book like this. But this sensitivity should be nurtured: there is too great a world in the films that raise questions and explore characters to pass up for a steady diet of movies and TV shows filled with stale cliches.

Organic unity comes in a film when all the parts fit together. The James Bond films, for all their technical polish, often are no more than episode strung onto episode, with little progression or unity. A film without organic unity can be good entertainment (NORTH BY NORTHWEST is a sprawling movie with many loose ends, but is great entertainment), but such a movie probably will not be a major achievement of film making.

film and novel

The most frequent source of movies—at least those made in this country—is the novel. Each year hundreds of novels become movies, and producers comb thousands more novels to find suitable stories for the screen. Throughout the history of movies there has been a close (though perhaps not always healthy) relationship between novels and films. Understanding a little about that relationship can reveal much about the nature of film —how it is like the novel, but also how it is distinct.

A case in point is the novel-become-film DOCTOR ZHIVAGO. Without a doubt, more Americans have seen the movie than have read the book—many more. Probably (as is often the case) many of those who had read the book first were disap-

tempts to project his sensitivity, his awareness of himself and the world about him, his acute sense of being alive. The novel, then, is very subjective, very personal; the author, Pasternak, was one of Russia's great poets, and Zhivago is a poet. Indeed, the volume concludes with selections of his poetry. The meaning of DOCTOR ZHIVAGO does not lie finally in the plot, in the interrelationships between characters, nor even in the panoramic view of history as reflected in the lives of several people. It lies in Zhivago, in the heart of Zhivago's life, which is his poetry. Here everything comes together, here the long, beautiful language in which the novel was written makes sense. And here is why the poems at the back of the volume are so

© 1966, Metro-Goldwyn-Mayer Inc., David Lean's Film DOCTOR ZHIVAGO

pointed in the movie, whereas those who hadn't read the book enjoyed it much more easily.

The book DOCTOR ZHIVAGO is a heavy, complex novel dealing with a long stretch of history and the effects of that period upon several people, most notably Yuri Andreyevich Zhivago. Zhivago is the center of the novel in many ways: the story follows his life; it depicts his relationship to his friends, his lover, his country; and finally, it at-

vitally important for the novel.

How, then, to make this novel into a film? David Lean, one of England's most competent directors, made the attempt. He used a wide screen and filmed the spectacular historical scenes and battles in impressive, bloody color. His composer, Maurice Jarre, wrote a beautiful score to help develop the love story between Zhivago and the magnificent Lara. Some of the best screen actors in Amer-

ica and England—Tom Courtenay, Rod Steiger, Julie Christie, Rita Tushingham—were chosen for major and minor roles. The film's budget totalled nearly 12 million dollars. Yet critics generally and viewers who had read the novel voiced disappointment. What had happened?

The fault may not have been with David Lean, or Robert Bolt, the writer, or with any of the cast, or anyone for that matter at the M.G.M. studios. Could anyone have made the novel DOCTOR ZHIVAGO into a truly successful film? Probably not. At its best and most characteristic moments the novel becomes poetry—pure language. These are the moments the movie simply cannot reproduce in filmic terms. There is one limping scene at Varykino, the country house in the Urals, where Zhivago gets up at night and writes a poem to his sleeping lover, Lara. We watch him attempt early versions of the poem, walk around distractedly, and finally write the poem—then we see the delight on Lara's face when she reads it. We never hear the poem, which is perhaps better—but the whole effect of the scene is sadly weak, compared with its power in the novel. If the film is supposed to center around Zhivago (and apparently it is), then it is a movie without a center, a movie filled with exciting drama and historical conflict at the periphery—but hollow within. We never really meet Zhivago in the film as we do in the novel; we never see life with his sensitivity, his intense awareness. Nor—and this is the important point—*could* we. DOCTOR ZHIVAGO is a novel, and a novel that doesn't contain the stuff of a film.

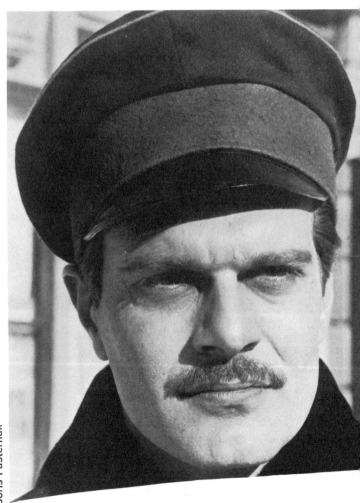

Boris Pasternak

130

© 1966, Metro-Goldwyn-Mayer Inc., scenes from David Lean's Film DOCTOR ZHIVAGO

DOCTOR ZHIVAGO is an extreme case. Most novels are not so bound to language as ZHIVAGO is, but many of them depend on effects that can be produced only by language and not really by film. John Fowles' novel THE COLLECTOR was made into a film—not a bad film, but much weaker in its statement than Fowles' novel. The story is simple: a butterfly collector, suddenly-become-rich, buys a remote country house in England. Then he kidnaps a co-ed art student and keeps her prisoner in the cellar. The novel is effective because it uses the technique of telling the story twice: once from the person of the young man, and again through the diary of the girl. Point of view here counts for everything: it charges the whole story with a clarity and a richness that could never be achieved in third-person narrative. But the camera cannot use the technique of shifting points of view. It must show everything, the whole action, as an outsider would see it. Right away the richness of the novel is stripped to a simple (if original) story. As a chilling horror story, THE COLLECTOR was handled well. But the movie suggests little of the psychological tension between the young man and the girl—a real if unavoidable loss.

There are many ways in which novels use language for effects that simply cannot be duplicated in filmic terms. The heavy, ponderous stream of consciousness in the novel CRIME AND PUNISH-MENT is for the most part lost in the film. TH DIARY OF A COUNTRY PRIEST reveals the agoni of a man's mind in words, but the film based o the novel is most effective when it uses faci expression, yet there it is much more limited.

The problem comes down to a basic differen in languages. Novels are conceived, thought ou and written in verbal language. Films are at lea executed (and the best are usually thought out) visual, or filmic language. Most of the great film did not come from novels; they originated as film The chance of an idea thought up for a film su ceeding as a film is probably better than th chance of a novel becoming a successful film. F a novel is dominated by language. It is most e pressive in using the potentialities of language. A film is dominated by the visual image and is most expressive in using the powers of the visual image.

This means, in effect, that a good novel is language centered; it may contain action, the makings of a valuable movie, but that is not the most important thing about it as a novel. Likewise, a movie may use dialogue brilliantly, but this, again, is not the most important thing about it as a film. A novel uses language—and a film uses the visual image. Language tends to be more personal, more subjective; it can search the interior of a character much more effectively and directly than a movie can. But a film can depict a dark street, a row of faces, any visual image more potently and directly than language can. The difference is important for understanding the film and the novel.

There are, then, some basic difficulties in making a novel into a film. This is not to say that it shouldn't be done—no doubt it will continue to be done. But the film maker should know the limits he faces and work with them. John Ford made one of the greatest films ever drawn from a novel, THE GRAPES OF WRATH. After the movie was completed and acclaimed as one of the best American films, Ford was asked how he did it.

"I NEVER READ THE BOOK!"

he said.

THE FILM AS FACT: THE DOCUMENTARY

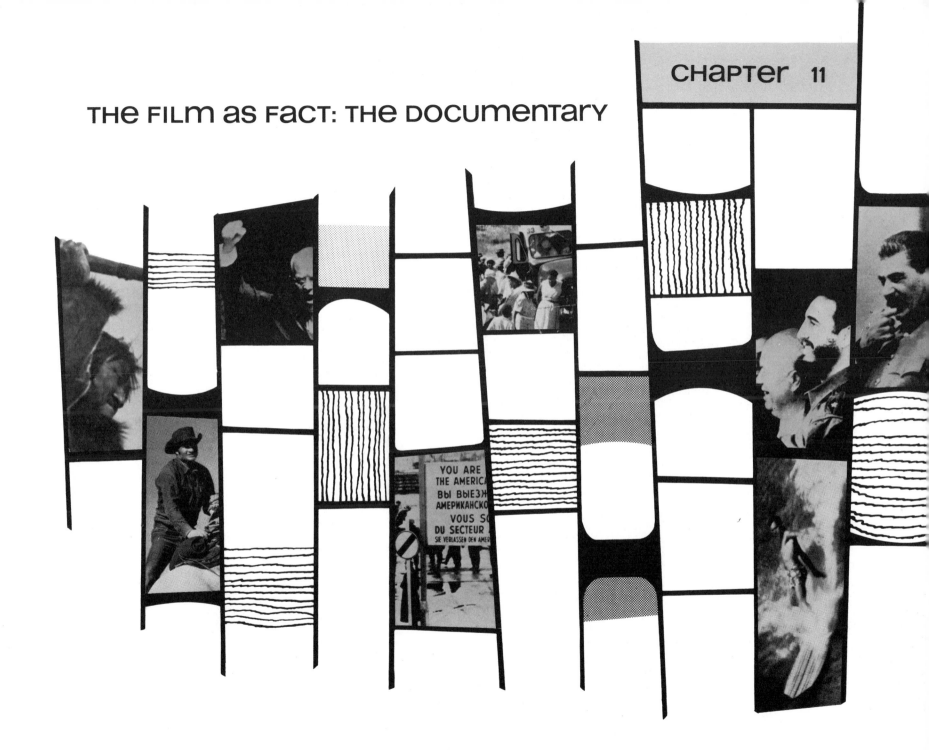

Robert Flaherty's NANOOK OF THE NORTH. Courtesy of Museum of Modern Art/Film Stills Archive

Almost 50 years ago, a young American explorer working for a mining firm in Northwest Canada was told he had done a good job and that he was to return home. Robert Flaherty, however, had no intentions of returning home. As an excuse to remain in the Hudson Bay area, among the Eskimo people he loved, he asked to make a film. Permission was granted, and Flaherty shot thousands of feet of film—only to have them burst into flames when he dropped a cigarette into them one day in the editing process.

Flaherty didn't stop. He begged to go back and finally was able to get a French firm Revillon Frères to sponsor a second attempt. This time Flaherty knew fairly clearly what he wanted. He would depict a year in the life of an Eskimo—but all the episodes would be filmed as the Eskimos lived them, and what "story" there was would grow from the drama of the Eskimos' struggle for survival.

Nanook was the Eskimo around whom Flaherty centered the film. A strong, courageous hunter, Nanook revealed the hidden nobility of the Eskimos' daring existence. Flaherty went with Nanook and photographed him hunting seals, fishing, building igloos, visiting the trading post, fighting the savage elements of the Far North. But in the finished movie these episodes take on a power and a magic beyond anything that could be suggested by words. NANOOK OF THE NORTH is a powerful, beautiful film in which every shot and every sequence brings out the drama of Nanook's life with reverence and force.

It took a while; but the film eventually became something of a success in America and abroad. People asked Flaherty how he had written such a simple and yet effective script, and Flaherty could only tell them that he had written no script, that he had let the lives of the Eskimos provide the script. He had simply followed behind, ready with his camera.

This concept of making a film—letting it emerge from the lives of the people being filmed—was somewhat revolutionary in 1922, when Flaherty made NANOOK. Yet it remains a key principle upon which the documentary film is based.

Flaherty never thought of himself as making any special kind of film. He admired the Eskimos and wanted to capture their lives on film as a tribute to their courage and nobility. NANOOK OF THE NORTH was his first movie. But the technique he used—so basically simple it could be called a lack of technique—was precisely to let life speak for itself, and not to impose some story or idea that wasn't already there.

NANOOK OF THE NORTH is not only one of the great classics of the documentary film; to this day it also remains one of the most superb and sympathetic treatments of a real man caught anywhere on film. Flaherty's cameras were early ones, and the quality of the film was not what it could have been today; nevertheless, Flaherty was able to create a film that has lasted, a film about man and nature much more powerful, honest, and profound than the many by Walt Disney or other film makers.

The basic difference between the documentary and the fiction film lies in the difference between the way Flaherty worked at NANOOK and the way a Hollywood studio goes about making a film. One comes out of real life, and the drama is dictated by the inherent conflict present; the other is imagined, created, acted out: the true creator is the film maker's imagination, not the people or events the film is about.

It could almost be said that the documentary film is a factual film. Almost—but not quite. Even if the story of Nanook's struggle emerges from Nanook's real life, there is still someone to determine what events of his life should be filmed and the camera angles from which these should be filmed. There is still someone to edit the film, to add commentary, to mold the living story of Nanook into a filmic story for the screen. In other words, the very making of a documentary film involves the insertion of someone's opinions, feelings, attitudes. The documentary is partly fact; it is also partly interpretation. John Grierson, one of the most important figures in the history of the documentary, once said, "You photograph the natural life, but you also, by your juxtaposition of detail, create an interpretation of it."

Interpretation (taking a fixed point of view) is almost inevitable in the documentary film. The film maker wants his final documentary to be dramatic, to come together with some unity and force. But the only way to do this is by interpreting or commenting on what he has shot as he puts it on the screen. NANOOK is not free of interpretation, but Flaherty's interpretation is such a sympathetic and honest one that we can hardly disagree with him.

Most documentaries don't set out simply to present real life with an interjected comment; they set out to convince the viewer of something.

If a man is about to make a documentary—say of the riots in an American city—he will probably not be satisfied simply to inform the viewer. Information can be gotten from newspapers and magazines; the power of a film is such that a film made simply to inform would be a dull film (in-

ructional films are a good example). Surely, most of a good documentary film will inform, but will inform in such a way that the viewer is ffected. This experience will lead, the film maker opes, to influence or convince the viewer.

An example: THE QUIET ONE. This sensitive, isturbing documentary was made in 1948 about Harlem slum child. Donald is 10 years old, a ictim of his father's desertion and his mother's ndifference. Shy, afraid, and terribly lonely, Donld runs—but there is nowhere, no one to run to. n anger he finally grabs a rock and tosses it hrough a store window. This brings Donald to ne Wiltwyck School for Boys, a place where he is eated with care and concern. The remainder of ne film shows Donald being brought out of him-elf, slowly and painfully, by the efforts of the Viltwyck staff. Although in the end the staff mem-

bers are not entirely successful, the film shows what progress they do make.

THE QUIET ONE is an extremely well-made documentary. Camera, movement, commentary, music: all the elements work together effectively, creating sympathy for Donald and a deep sense of the human crisis Donald is experiencing. The film surely is factual: Donald's case represents hundreds seen by the Wiltwyck staff and the staffs of similar schools every year. And the shots of Harlem, Donald's mother, the Wiltwyck School are all highly authentic and highly realistic.

But the film also seeks to persuade, to convince. Our feelings toward Harlem are a little different after this film: we feel that human loneliness can be a disease more crippling than paralysis; we become convinced of the profound need each man experiences for another person's love. We feel

convinced of these things, however, not because the film has preached to us (it does a remarkable job of avoiding preaching, for a film with this theme), but because the documentary story of Donald—depicted as it is in the film—compels us to realize his need for love. The film, while remaining an honest documentary, has been persuasive.

There is a great persuasive power in honesty. And if NANOOK and THE QUIET ONE, both highly persuasive documentaries, share any feature, it is their profound honesty. Both of them, admittedly, had to "stage" certain scenes: when Nanook catches a walrus through the ice, it is already dead; and Donald and the Wiltwyck School officials acted out a few of the scenes in the film. Yet both films began with real life; both were reverent and honest toward their subjects, and both drew totally from the life of their subjects.

A scene from the National Film Board of Canada production THE RUNNER

Scenes from the National Film Board of Canada production CORRAL

This method, with its persuasive power, is enormously different from the technique used in a propagandistic documentary like Hitler's TRIUMPH OF THE WILL, in which camera effects are used to create illusions and strong feelings.

Looking at the vast number of documentaries made over the years, there are probably no guidelines for filming a documentary other than the one that guided Flaherty in making NANOOK: to draw the story, the shots, the theme from the events or the people themselves. This leaves an enormous range in which documentaries can be made—so much so that the chilling film NIGHT AND FOG, depicting the horrors of Germany's concentration camps, would be a documentary, as would such Canadian films as RUNNER (a poetic short about a long-distance runner) and CORRAL (a simple, though beautifully made, story of a man corralling and saddling a wild horse).

There is almost no limit to the subjects treated in documentaries. UNIVERSE is an astronomer's view of the galaxies and nebulae: a powerful film by any standards. HARVEST OF SHAME, a television documentary depicting the tragic plight of migrant farmers in America, consists largely of interviews; yet these are handled creatively enough to remain constantly alive. Recent experimental documentaries, such as END OF SUMMER, endeavor to make as little comment or interpretation as possible. They simply follow their subjects around and show what the subjects do and say. The effect is strange but fascinating.

Despite the great number of documentaries that have been made and their frequent use in television, the documentary is still not a highly popular form of film. In recent years only a handful of them were able to break into the commercial theater markets (ENDLESS SUMMER; YEARS OF LIGHTNING, DAY OF DRUMS; and THE WAR GAME are three). When they appear on television, though they attract a large audience, it is usually not

Scenes from the National Film Board of Canada production END OF SUMMER

Cinema V Distributing, Inc., a Bruce Brown production ENDLESS SUMMER

141

HARVEST OF SHAME, produced by David Lowe. Courtesy of Contemporary Films, Inc.

nearly so large as those attracted by the typical series shows.

Nevertheless, the documentary can do much that the fiction film cannot. It can reveal man's world—and man—with a searching honesty difficult, if not impossible, to achieve in the fiction film. Movies like HARVEST OF SHAME and LET MY PEOPLE GO reveal the tragedy of persecuted people with an almost devastating force. Documentaries have a directness about them that can only be achieved in the fiction film through the use of documentary methods. ON THE WATERFRONT and NOBODY WAVED GOODBYE are both fiction films, but to convey a sharp sense of reality they employ techniques of the documentary film—shooting real people (both used non-actors in their normal occupations), real places (both were shot almost entirely outside of studios), and real situations (both were drawn from authentic situations).

John Grierson once said that "the materials and the stories thus taken from the raw can be finer than the acted article. Spontaneous gesture has a special value on the screen. Cinema has a sensational capacity for enhancing the movement which tradition has formed or time worn smooth." Anyone who has seen a purely spontaneous gesture in a film—whether Nanook biting on a record to see if it could be eaten, or Peter Mark thumbing his nose at a parking-lot customer in NOBODY WAVED GOODBYE—knows how convincing, and how right, such moments can be in the film. These moments usually cannot come from a fiction film; most actors are under too much stress to be really spontaneous. But the documentary film (as well as live or taped television) can bring out spontaneity—a quality people today want.

143

The expressive range of the documentary is broad. It is one field of the film (like the animated film) that has hardly been tapped and which needs much exploration. Most documentaries are made with the same pattern and the same flaws: a simple "story" (or event) in which the commentary dominates, not the visual drama. One has only to see a few superb documentaries (NANOOK, LET MY PEOPLE GO, and THE QUIET ONE are three) to be able to see through the phoniness and shoddiness of most of the others.

People will probably not *like* documentaries as much as they like typical feature films or television serials. But then, most documentaries aren't made simply to be liked. They are made to be seen and, generally, to be taken seriously. The potential of the documentary lies in the field of social criticism and of depicting and interpreting events and people. To neglect the documentary would be to neglect one of the most potent expressions that film has found or is likely to find.

say it with film

We have been saying that film is, above all, a language—and any language exists in order to communicate. This chapter will look at *what* films communicate: the ideas, meanings, and themes of movies.

Often the most potent question that can be asked about a feature film is, What was its theme? What was it trying to say? The answer is sometimes obvious and simple: ALL THE WAY HOME describes a ten-year-old boy's experience of his father's death. The film was made with taste and great sympathy; the theme is simply the effect of a father's death on a young boy. But in other films the theme can be more complex, more difficult to reach and fully understand. NOTHING BUT A MAN describes the efforts of a Southern Negro Duff Anderson to keep a job and his self-respect at the same time. He loses his job—in fact, one job after another—because he will not submit to the degradation to which other Negroes submit. Finally he runs away from his wife—only to encounter his father, who had been running all his life, and watches him destroy himself. The sobering experience sends Duff back to his wife with sharper self-understanding and renewed courage.

A Cinema V Presentation, NOTHING BUT A MAN, A Roemer-Young Du-Art Production. Courtesy of Film Center, Inc.

What exactly is the theme of NOTHING BUT A MAN? On one level it appears to be the struggle of one man to live as a man, as the master of his own fate. On another level it appears to be the paralyzing failure at the heart of the Negro family: the wife can work and be successful when the husband can't. On yet another level, the theme of the film could be interpreted in terms of the deadlock that Southern whites have on Southern Negroes. Is any one the theme? Are all three aspects of a larger theme? When a film attempts to deal with a complex social or personal problem, its theme will invariably be complex and will probably work on several levels.

Any effort to become sensitive to movies will involve a greater perceptiveness of a film's theme and the way in which that theme is expressed. In the first chapter, NOBODY WAVED GOODBYE, the story of a Canadian boy and girl who run away from home, was described. Viewers can see this movie and remain oblivious to any questions about the nature of freedom and constraint—a theme which dominates the film. Peter runs away from home because he wants his freedom; but by short-changing parking-lot customers and finally by stealing money and a car, he reveals that for the sake of freedom he has sold himself into a greater slavery. Not only is the theme strong in NOBODY WAVED GOODBYE, but the way in which it is expressed, through words, situations, facial expres-

sions, images, and music also shows that the director was highly conscious of what he was doing in making the film.

Films like NOTHING BUT A MAN and NOBODY WAVED GOODBYE develop complex and well-treated themes, and by treating these themes skillfully they raise questions and spur thought.

Movies are not notorious for stimulating thought. The popular image (and there is some truth to it) is that they do just the opposite. Ad mittedly, the way in which a film works—going from the visual image directly to the viewer and his emotions—is different from the way in which books work. As we read a book we are constantly, in a sense, thinking. But as we watch a film (especially a film that is hardly demanding), we don't have to think. We can just sit back and "enjoy ourselves."

The danger is, of course, that after seeing a film we won't bother thinking about it at all. It will have been an experience, a fun or dull one. But it's over. And yet it isn't. Many films, especially many recent ones, were written and made with something to say. Films like GRAND PRIX, IN COLD BLOOD, A MAN FOR ALL SEASONS, and WHO'S AFRAID OF VIRGINIA WOOLF? deal with serious themes. And these themes are not automatically understood simply by watching the movies. They demand thought. They have raised questions that people should think about and often be disturbed by. What do the cars do to the men who drive them in GRAND PRIX? Why did the Clutter murders, depicted so realistically in the grim movie IN COLD BLOOD, ever have to happen?

Very often the best films are those that do demand thought and leave the viewer with unanswered questions. This does not mean these films cannot be entertaining. DOCTOR STRANGELOVE, OR HOW I LEARNED TO STOP WORRYING AND LOVE THE BOMB is at times a hilarious film. But the story is not: a general with the power to drop bombs over Russia has gone berserk and orders the bombs dropped. The President discovers this and, only after a long struggle, is able to order all the planes back—except for one. The finale of the film is a combination of grim statement about the self-destructiveness of man and pure farce; a kind of black humor. The film is—well, not thoroughly, but largely—enjoyable. Yet it raises some stinging, very disturbing questions about the existence of nuclear bombs and the constant temptation to do something with them.

© 1963, Columbia Pictures. Scenes from Stanley Kubrick's DR. STRANGELOVE

I WANT TO LIVE is a film based on the life of Barbara Graham, a convicted murderess who pleaded innocence every step of the way to the gas chamber. The film is a powerful suspense thriller, made with a gritty realism which convinces the viewer that this actually happened. While the film does not say that Graham was innocent, it at the same time doesn't suggest that she was guilty. The question is left open to severe doubt. We see only her frantic efforts to convince lawyers, newspapermen, the public that she never killed anyone. Finally she is able to convince one of the journalists who originally pressed for her guilt—a Pulitzer Prize-winning newspaperman, who in real life was responsible for making the movie. With his help things begin to look somewhat hopeful; the execution is deferred briefly, but not for long enough time. The cameras watch the two lab technicians unplug the jar with the cyanide capsule and test the latch on the door of the gas chamber. Every moment leading up to Barbara Graham's execution is felt with a chilling personal involvement. At her death the movie stops and the viewer walks away, like the stunned journalist, asking himself questions which perhaps he never asked himself before. I WANT TO LIVE questions, the best way a movie can question, such things as the tendency of the press to "try" a defendant, capital punishment, and the possibility of the court's condemning people "by mistake."

Any movie that attempts honestly and maturely to come to grips with life is going to raise questions. It is going to deal with a theme worth thinking about—whether the classic themes of love and violence, or the more contemporary themes of race relations, or the responsibility of the press not to influence the conviction of a defendant.

This doesn't mean that films without strong, provocative themes are weak; they are simply limited. Hollywood long ago learned the formulas for making movies for pure entertainment and escape, and it has been reluctant ever since to make much else. Entertainment can be one of the major purposes of film; but if it becomes the single purpose of film, with movie makers ignoring all the possible themes they could tap, then movies are doomed to a frightening sterility. Unfortunately, television has come to be thought of almost strictly in terms of escapist entertainment. Serious drama, the exploration of important social themes: these do not seem to be too attractive to television programmers. The same has been largely true of films made in this country for a great number of years.

In the fiction, or feature film, a theme is relatively easy to pursue. We know there is a theme, and through the situation, characters, and action we are brought to recognize it: whether the effects of disloyalty in the criminal underground or a man's need to be free. There is another way in which themes—or more accurately, meanings—can be dealt with in films. We may not be asked to search out a theme; on the contrary, the theme is communicated to us—but incognito. We have learned what the film maker wanted us to learn, but are not quite aware that we have learned it. This is film comment through propaganda.

Propaganda is the conscious effort on the part of someone to change our attitudes about something—only not through clear logical processes, such as we employ in learning at school. Propaganda uses, instead, the power of suggestion, feeling, prejudice.

The word *propaganda* is usually associated with Hitler's Germany or modern-day China. Wherever there are people trying to change other people's attitudes, however, there is probably propaganda.

152

Advertising—and especially television commercials—is loaded with propaganda. Documentary films, noted for their seeming objectivity, often attempt subtly not simply to inform, but to inform in such a way that the viewer's reactions will be what the film maker wants. War films, for example, generally depict the Germans as brutish combat-mongers and the Japanese as grinning, well-groomed savages. Propaganda.

Propaganda is hard to notice in the press; it is even harder to spot in films. Movies convey, at least on the surface, a tremendous sense of being real. A documentary film, made from actual events and living people, especially seems to be real, unfaked; yet this can often be the most potent for propaganda purposes. During the 1930's, when Hitler was trying to get the German people totally behind him, he had a "documentary" film made about the Third Reich, a movie called TRIUMPH OF THE WILL. This film centers on a large Party rally, but attempts to engage the viewer in a frenzy of feeling and loyalty to Hitler. The cameras scan faces at the Nuremburg rallies, showing the faces becoming more and more excited. The editing adds to the excitement, and the camera, always in movement, gives the entire film a sense of total movement, total change—a feeling that Hitler wanted to see in the German people. Camera angles speak too: shots are taken looking up at the Reich eagle, symbol of the government; but the next shot is of Hitler, at an even steeper angle, with the sky a broad frame behind him. The effect of such techniques is to suggest a great deal more than the viewer (at least the viewer at that time) would consciously realize.

Films will always be used for propagandistic purposes. How successful such films will be depends on the maturity and perceptiveness of the viewers. Television commercials, probably the most obvious form of propaganda, often are not effective propaganda simply because we expect them to try to change our attitudes and we resist. Propaganda works best when we don't expect it —when we think we are getting honesty and forthright communication.

153

Movies speak. And it is important to know not only the language in which they can speak best but also what they are saying. The full experience of a movie demands the attempt to understand, to question the meaning the film maker had in mind. For the film, finally, is not about camera angles or editing; it is about man and who man is. The gaunt, heroic Eskimo Nanook stands poised with his spear ready in NANOOK OF THE NORTH. This shot was not taken because it was a good-looking shot—it was taken because it reveals the manhood, the strength, the power of Nanook. And that —the understanding of Nanook and finally of man —is what movies are all about.

NANOOK OF THE NORTH. Courtesy of Museum of Modern Art/Film Stills Archive

FILM CRITICISM

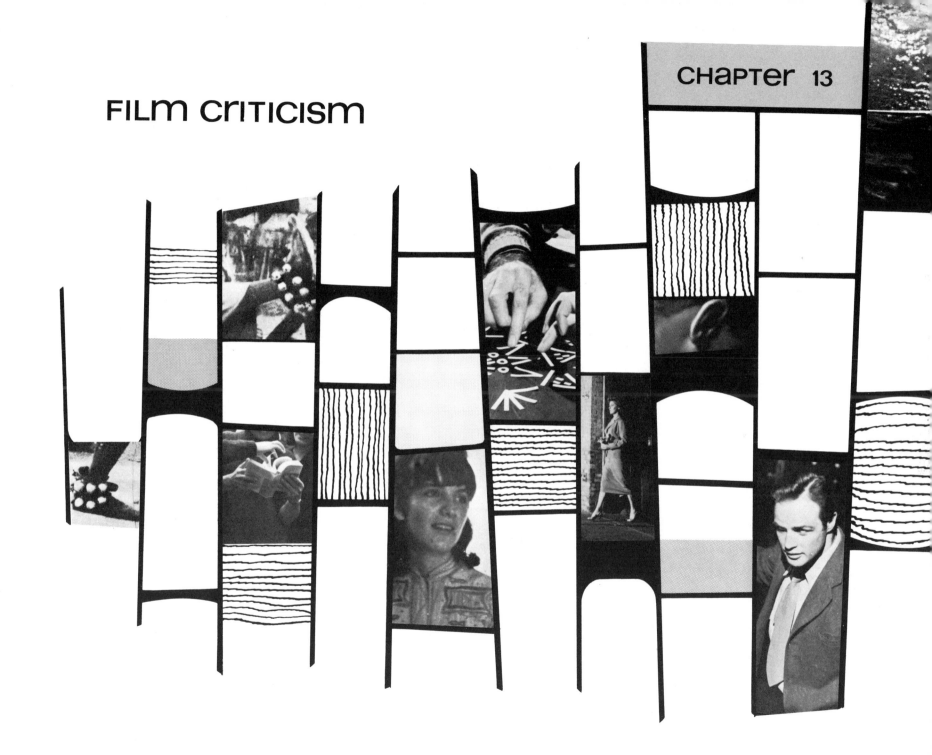

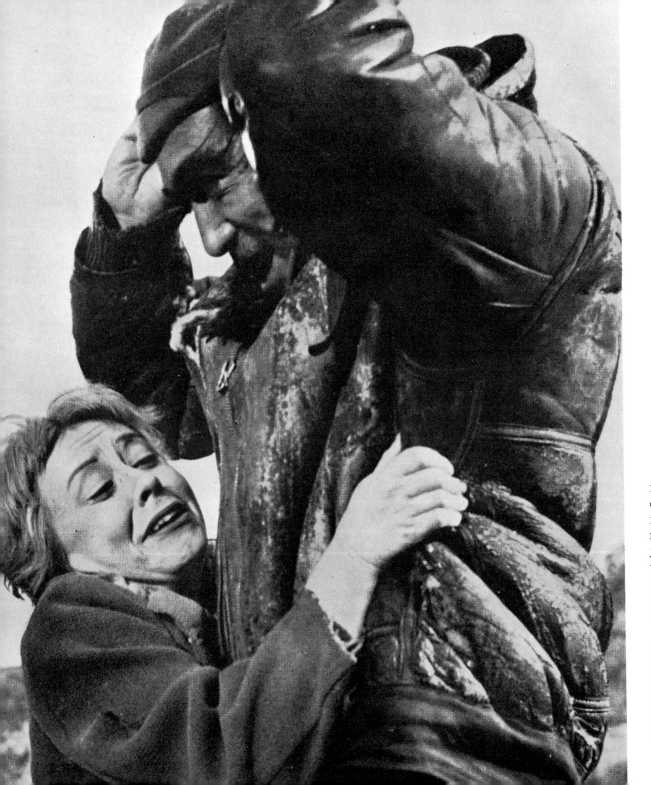

All that has been said up to now should have le in two directions: toward a better understandin of film language and toward a better understan ing of the actual use of filmic language in th making of films. This second direction, perhap just as important as the first, is covered in Cha ter 15, "To Make a Film.'" The first directio however, is not such a clear one. When do w know filmic language? When can we see, really se a movie?

Admittedly, we have seen a movie and unde stood it when we can identify its theme, when has stimulated feeling and thought. The Italia film LA STRADA centers around a pathetic girl wh is dominated by a bestial circus strongman, Zan pano. Throughout the film we feel with the gi sense her loneliness and emptiness, her feelin that she doesn't mean anything to anyone. Event

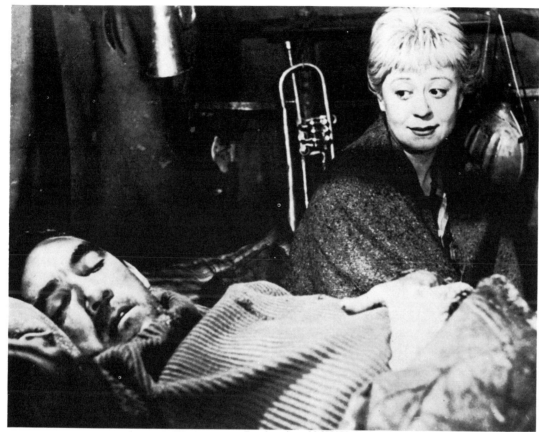

lly she dies, and the film closes with Zampano's iscovery of her death. LA STRADA is a moving, isturbing film, but also a beautiful one. To over-ear someone walking away from it with the com-nent, "I don't see why he got so bothered at the nd," or "I thought it was a pretty dull movie," or So what?" suggests that some viewers were not ally seeing LA STRADA. They have eyes, but they o not see.

It is not necessary that we agree on the quality f a movie or perhaps even the theme; there are uestions that even the best films leave open to dis-cussion. It is necessary, though, that we be open to feel what a good movie wants us to feel, that we be delighted, or upset, titillated, or disturbed by a movie. With a well-made movie, seeing is feeling; there is no difference. To know filmic lan-guage does not mean that a viewer concentrates on the types of editing or watches to make sure each shot is composed effectively. The knowledge of filmic language should become so much a part of viewing a movie that the viewer isn't conscious of applying it as he watches. He simply watches, and feels.

The question is still unanswered: when does a person really know film language? When is he capable of drawing from a film all that is there? The best guideline here is an explanation which has seen a thousand uses, yet which still carries meaning: when a person is capable of intelligent criticism.

Film criticism doesn't mean that someone gripes about everything he didn't like in a film. Many of the things people don't like in films (for example, the slow pace of some recent European films) actually help the films, make them better movies. Film criticism also doesn't mean writing a column in a magazine or newspaper; this is one form of film criticism, but not all there is to it.

Criticism is the ability to judge with intelligence, feeling, and above all with accuracy the

Scenes from the National Film Board of Canada production END OF SUMMER

quality of a film. The focus in criticism is the film. The man who says, "I didn't like that movie" and goes on to list the reasons why he didn't like it may be on the road to being a film critic—but he isn't one yet. On the other hand, the man who says, "It was a strong movie with good photography, but it had a weak plot," comes much closer. He is concerned primarily with the movie, not with the way he felt about it.

True, the way we feel about a movie may be one of our best guides to a criticism of the film. But to base criticism strictly on personal reaction can be narrow. The real critic should be able to say that in spite of his dislike for a certain movie, it remains a great or important film.

What, then, are the guidelines to film criticism? Certainly personal reaction should be one: after all, this was what the film was made for, that we could experience it, not so we could sit back and analyze it. Indeed, we shouldn't analyze everything we see, only (and this is the important point) be capable of it.

The first guideline should be an awareness of what the film maker was trying to do. END OF SUMMER is a half-hour-long movie about a camp in Canada. It is the last week, and we watch the teen-age girls at the camp discuss personal questions, swim and boat, completely enjoying themselves. There is no story, no very obvious theme: simply the beauty of this last week in August. Numerous viewers have probably seen END OF SUMMER and felt acute disappointment; no story, no real character development, no clear continuity —only the creation of a powerful mood. Yet the film maker Michel Brault wasn't attempting a story, character, or theme: he wanted to see how much of the feeling of that last week could be caught on film. And to criticize END OF SUMMER without at least this recognition would be to miss the point of the film.

Understanding the film maker's purpose in a film is not easy; it calls for a heightened attentiveness, an openness that does not demand of a movie something the movie will not have. Experimental films, such as Len Lye's or Norman McLaren's sketching directly onto the film, do not even involve images—only lines and blots. Again, what was the film maker trying to do? Many of these experimental films, such as FIDDLE-DEE-DEE and SERENAL, achieve some fascinating rhythms between the moving scratches and the music. Any responsive viewer should realize that this is the purpose in the film and not look for more, or even be disappointed that there is not more.

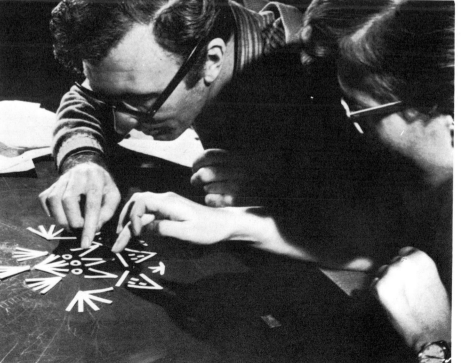

Scene from the National Film Board of Canada production LE MERLE, film artist Norman McLaren

Another guideline: the film maker had an ide in mind, but how did he express it? In imaginativ filmic language? Or in clichés? There are differer ways of handling any story, any scene, any sho And those ways that bring out the inner qualit of, say, a shot, the most incisive camera angl the most effective and original line, the most subt editing, are probably going to use filmic langua much more potently than a shot that has been use dozens of times before. Films are filled with stoc moments—moments when it seems a shot or scer was taken right out of another movie, or man other movies. The running fugitive meets tl young girl; the police chief insists on getting h man; or in commercials, brand A washes cleane than brand B. The use of filmic language in ori inal, creative ways is a must for a good film. Pov erful plays have been made into films, and rema powerful experiences, but not powerful films.

A third major guideline: when a movie uses filmic language, is the language very expressive? TOM JONES is a movie filled with camera tricks: fast motion, superfast editing, zoom-ins and zoom-outs. But critics have challenged the movie, saying that all these camera effects do not express the fundamental concern of the movie. Filmic language is like any language: it can be overused, become florid and heavy. The effective use of any language depends upon a careful selection of vocabulary and a controlled use of structures. If a barroom brawl is filmed at a distance from a fixed camera angle (rather than from the center of the brawl, with fast-paced editing), filmic language is probably not being used as it could or should. The difference is significant.

GUIDELINES|RULES ▶

These three guidelines, then (and they are no more than guidelines), can direct some kind of critical reaction to films: What was the film maker's purpose? Did he use filmic language creatively? And where he used filmic language, was it expressive?

for film criticism are on the following two pages

There are really no rules, no clear answers to the making of a sensitive filmgoer. No one can teach aliveness, openness, or love, and worthwhile film viewing is not only like these things, it also involves these things. Sensitivity to good films is probably cultivated best by seeing good films, really seeing them—and thinking, talking, perhaps even writing about them afterward.

One person who can make possible more sensitive filmgoing is the professional movie critic, the one who writes about films in magazines and newspapers. Now, many strong things can be said against movie critics, especially the local critics who write for city newspapers. And no one should surrender his attitudes about a movie to what a critic says. Indeed, half the fun of having critics is being able to disagree with them. But the movie critics who write columns do offer one thing (at least some of them do): the example of a sensitive, acute eye.

When someone goes to see a film, he sees only part of what happens on the screen. Any discussion after a movie reveals that no two persons' experience of a movie is exactly alike. There is too much in a movie to get everything out of one showing; and besides, we all bring to a film our own background, feelings, and attitudes. Yet some people are able to get more out of a movie than others —and some of the professional critics can be helpful simply because they do get more out of movies and tell us about it.

The role of the critic should be to make us more attentive, to make us see better. And if we listen to the best of them, they will enable us to do just this. Of course, the critics may (and invariably do) argue among themselves about the final quality of a film, demonstrating that sometimes nobody knows for sure. Yet in describing films and in casting their judgments upon films, they can be most helpful in bringing us to sense better, to see better, to feel better—and to make more exact judgments ourselves.

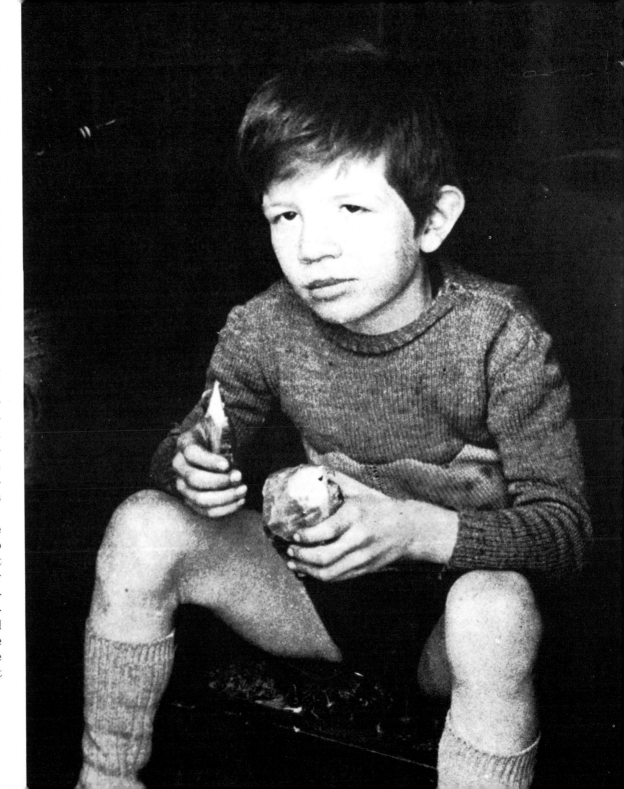

Le Film d'Art production, CHILDREN ADRIFT. Courtesy of Contemporary Films, Inc.

Television

There is an anecdote about some people on a British beach. Everyone in the area sat with his back to the sea, clustered around a little hut. In the hut a television set was on; the picture: the sea.

This is an exaggeration, of course, but statistics show that the amount of time people spend watching television alone makes a discussion of TV important. As a national average in America, people spend more time watching television than doing anything else, except sleeping.

The whole subject of television is naturally too big for what can be said in a chapter. Yet most of us spend more time watching television than watching movies in a theater, and it is important to recognize that the way the little electronic box affects us is different from the way in which the big screen and dark hall of a theater affect us.

Whatever we see on television—whether an installment of a ragged, tear-jerking soap opera or a powerful movie on the late, late show—comes to us in a different way than in the theater. For one thing, television is generally broken up into fragments. A drama or series show is chopped into about four or five parts by commercials. And each commercial jerks us away from the show, keeps us from becoming as involved as we could if the show went right through without interruption. Then again, as we pointed out before, the environment is different. In a theater, there is nothing we see *but* the picture: everything else is dark; the picture is our environment. But a television show is almost never the whole environment. The screen is only part of a bigger environment—and usually an environment in which distractions are frequent. These distractions, like commercials, keep television watching from becoming the involving experience that film watching in a theater can be. Or put it this way: the kind of involvement is different.

This basic difference in the way we experience theater, movies, and television can help us understand what sort of drama—or indeed, what sort of show—is best fitted for a small TV set, and what sort of drama is best fitted for the large

screen. Television can bring out personal qualities and personality much more quickly and effectively than a movie. And with its live and entertaining guest shows, television lends itself to spontaneous expression rather than rehearsed activity. The success of such personalities as Johnny Carson and the Smothers Brothers—highly spontaneous entertainers—shows how television is fitted for natural expression. One critic has commented that TV produced more hams than Armour's; the comparison may be corny, but it is true.

Television is made to the scale of a person, and any film on television, for example, a series show, will be most successful if it concentrates on close-up shots and brings out the full presence of its actors. "Mission: Impossible," to mention one well-made television show (there aren't a large number), uses almost no other shot than the close-up, but the cutting is so quick and so deftly handled that the viewer is hardly aware of the pre-

dominance of close-ups. A film shown on a large screen, however, can use long shots and medium shots much more frequently—simply because we are still capable of seeing what happens out on the desert or inside the saloon. If those movies are eventually shown on the late show, all we can see is a desert with little things scooting around in the background, or men in a saloon whom we can't distinguish.

The major difference between television and movies, however, is the basic nature of television. It is an electronic device that enables a picture to be sent over the air or on a cable into any possible number of homes. Any picture is possible, and while films are a major source of television programming, they are not the entire source. Sports, political conventions, panels, and quiz programs are often shown live, or on a recent (perhaps made 6 to 10 hours earlier) videotape recording. This means that film is only one aspect of tele-

vision: and that the use of film here is best limited to the expressive potential of television as a medium.

What is this expressive potential? It is hard to define for several reasons. Television, to begin with, is still young: only 20 years old; it has not had the chance to explore its potential as the movies have (which have been around over 70 years). The way in which television developed, as an outgrowth of radio and not with a totally fresh start (as movies and radio both had), retarded its progress in developing in its own right. But perhaps most crucial has been the commercial control of the television networks; this control has, especially over the last 10 years, discouraged experiment and innovation and has insisted much more strongly upon a guaranteed large audience than a well-produced, effective show.

A sketchy understanding of the history of television can be very helpful here. Technically, the

complex electronic device we call television was 131 years in the making. In 1817 a Swedish professor discovered that *selenium,* a substance drawn from sulphur, could be used to carry electricity. Later discoveries enabled scientists to convey light through electrical charges. In 1920 the experimentation moved from private laboratories to the wealthy corporations like General Electric and especially the Radio Corporation of America. The fact that the Radio Corporation of America played a significant role in developing television would prove to be decisive in shaping the history of the television as a medium. Radio people—men trained to work with voices and sounds—would be the leaders in young television.

The first actual telecast took place on April 7, 1927; from that point on, television was technically possible though not economically feasible. A few industrial and closed-circuit uses were made of television in the very early years, but nothing which led to open broadcasting. For a number of years a few broadcasts were made, picked up only by amateur TV hobbyists and the very few people who had early sets. In 1936 the British Broadcasting Corporation attempted some telecasts, but sets, retailing at about $300 each, just did not sell. Americans who had been experimenting with television agreed that the time was not yet ripe, and David Sarnoff, one of the key figures in the development of television (he later headed NBC), said that television would not be ready until 1939. He was right. Late in April, 1939, the first telecast went on the air and sets went on sale to the public.

Television programming over the next seven or eight years was in its very early experimental stage. Top radio performers became a key television attraction, and attempts were made to broadcast news directly from the spot. World War II slowed down the number of sets sold and the programming, but the technical innovations made during the war—especially the developments in radar—proved to be extremely important for the development of television.

After the war, America was ready for television. Sets went on sale again, but sold out more rapidly than the manufacturers could supply them. In 1947 the early "big programs" began going on the air, programs such as "Meet the Press," and "Howdy Doody." In 1948 (the year in which most television people believe commercial TV was actually born), 25 new stations began operating throughout the country. This same year was also significant because TV finally began showing a profit. All the time it had been spending money and regaining little of it; finally it was reaping more money than was being put into it.

By 1950 there were 100 stations operating and 4 major networks (DuMont, which has since collapsed, ABC, NBC, and CBS). Television, now operating on a full daytime and evening schedule, had become big business and a more and more compulsory part of every American home. Aside from the struggle to develop color television, the growth after 1950 was primarily numerical growth: the number of sets owned by Americans, the number of stations operating, the number of hours spent viewing television daily.

American television, from its beginning, followed the commercial system that dominated radio. This meant that air time was "purchased" by a sponsor much as magazine space would be purchased for an advertisement. As the networks grew, however, the method became more complex. A show made in New York costs hundreds of thousands of dollars. The network does not pay for the program; it simply makes sure that it is broadcast and available to local stations all over the country at whatever time it goes on. With the knowledge that almost every local station will pick up the show, a sponsor (or combination of sponsors) will pay for the program. But how do they know they are getting their money's worth? The stakes in television advertising are high, enormously high. A quarter of a million dollars might easily be spent for all the expenses in a single episode of an expensively made serial like "Bonanza." For a sponsor to spend all this money, uncertain of how many people are being affected by the commercials, would be economic suicide.

Television, therefore, has spawned a remarkable method of "locating" audience size: the ratings. The ratings are easily one of the most controversial aspects of commercial television—and understandably so. On the basis of what shows 1,000 people (contacted by the rating system) are watching, estimates are made about the millions of people watching television at that time. These estimates spell the life or death of almost every show that goes on television.

The people who take the ratings (Nielsen is the best known) do not claim to be exactly right; nor do the sponsors admit that the ratings offer an exact mathematical account. If 50 million sets are on in an evening, a hundred families are contacted during a half hour, and the breakdown is 40, 33, and 27 percent, no one would claim that the exact breakdown of audiences would be 20, 16½, or 13 million—they would merely agree that these numbers give them a valid idea where the audiences of the shows stand in relationship to one another.

How valid is this? Experts in statistics say that there would not be a very large difference between contacting a carefully chosen 100 or 10,000. Yet it is on the basis of this 100, realistically, that a show survives or dies. A show that draws only 20 million viewers when its two competitors are attracting 27 million and 30 million has scarcely any chance of staying on the air—no matter if it is stimulating drama, important political comment, or what.

The rating system may seem like a serious failure at the heart of the present television system. Actually, ratings are only symptomatic of the very structure of commercial television. If a sponsor backs a show it is with the idea of promoting his product to as many individual television viewers as possible. If a show simply doesn't attract that many people, no matter how good it may be, it has precious little chance of staying on the air. Commercial television basically has no room for minorities: the financial expense demands that every show be able to engage the largest audience possible.

There are alternative systems by which televi-

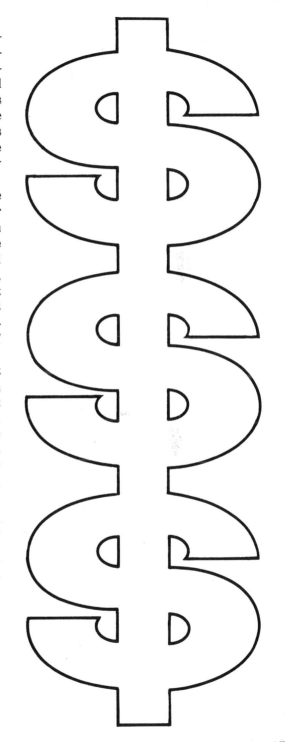

sion could operate. Total commercial broadcasting is used only in very few countries; most (as with the British Broadcasting Corporation) use government funds. Pay television, although not in wide use anywhere right now, has been suggested as a good way to get more specialized entertainment on the air.

The only present alternative to commercial television in this country is public, or educational, television.

Public television, sponsored by the large foundations and just recently by the Federal Government, is yet in its infancy. Some of the shows run on public television stations have been exceptionally good; more often than not, however, they tend to be teachy and dull—largely because public television doesn't have the money to attract top talent. Yet the future of public television looks particu-

larly bright, for the commercial stations have been convincing viewers of their bankruptcy in providing stimulating programming, and people may turn increasingly to their only other option: public TV.

During the brief history of television, several different forms have emerged, which we today identify as the basic TV listings. Some of these forms are the serial drama, the live coverage of sports or news events, the quiz and giveaway shows, the news program, the discussion show. Three—the dramatic or comedy serial, the coverage of live events, and the news program or special documentary—are worthy of comment, for they provide the most typical and critical forms of television fare.

The television series program is the most familiar type of television show. The idea of returning each week (or in some cases twice a week)

with the same actors, roughly the same situation, the same plot structure, and the same tone was actually inherited from radio, where series like "The Shadow" and "The Lone Ranger" were once extremely popular. The radio series had the same characters returning to fight in a similar situation through each episode. Listeners always knew who would win, who was the bad guy and who was the good guy; but they returned every week in ever increasing numbers. Early television successes like "Dragnet," "Big Story," and "The Lone Ranger" followed the same pattern. One show would establish not only what the characters were like, but how the plot would unfold, what sort of opponents the hero(es) would face, what tone the show would have (contrast the grim realism of "Dragnet" with the mock style of "Batman"), just about everything except some minor adjustments in the plot

Adele Pacacios in RUN, APPALOOSA, RUN; WALT DISNEY'S WONDERFUL WORLD OF COLOR. Courtesy, NBC Television

Jayne Meadows and Red Skelton, THE RED SKELTON SHOW. Courtesy, CBS Television

Julian Bream, BELL TELEPHONE HOUR. Courtesy of NBC Television

173

S·E·R·I·E·S

Bernard Bresslaw and Patrick McGoohan in SECRET AGENT. Courtesy, CBS Television

Even the structure of the plot remains the same. "Secret Agent" was a television series made in England in which the plot was built totally around complications. John Drake, the secret agent, would run into major complications in each episode, causing him to rethink everything and act quickly on the spot. The suspense each show could build this way was rare in television. "Mission: Impossible," the show that followed "Secret Agent," dealt with roughly the same theme: this time a team of men, rather than a single agent, attempted highly risky assignments. "Mission: Impossible" achieves potent suspense, but with a completely different plot pattern. Phelps and his team learn their assignment and plan each step with care and precision. The whole show consists of watching the plan unfold; there never are real complications (some near-complications, as the near discovery of an agent's being in disguise, but never anything that alters the Plan). Both shows are highly successful television suspense dramas. But both work within a tight framework—the same characters, the same theme, roughly the same situation, and the same kind of plot.

What makes the television series work? Why are there so few original dramas and almost no weekly shows that present different dramas? The series show is built on the psychology of expectation. People tend to turn on a set if they know what they are about to see. For them to be sure that the show will be well handled is not enough; they want to know who will act, how he will act, what the situation will be, what the humor will be like, or what the plot will be like. Consequently, the series show is bound to be more popular than the original drama—if, unfortunately, less original and less demanding of its audience.

One of the great values of television is its ability to bring viewers instantaneous coverage of important events. The nation, for example, suddenly became a united, thinking, feeling people the weekend after John F. Kennedy's assassination. Television enabled citizens everywhere to participate in the grief, the shock, the recognition of the President's death. Political conventions, the debates of political figures vying for office, on-the-spot coverage of important meetings as in the U.N.: all these are possible through television. The distance between a citizen and the important decisions of his leaders is suddenly shrunk by the power of television coverage; likewise, suddenly there is the ability to see history happen.

Not only can television provide news as it happens: it can report and interpret that news quickly. Recent polls show that most people get their news from television and radio rather than from newspapers. Although sponsors have never been able to support the large expenses involved in procuring and reporting news, the networks have considered one of their major functions as providing honest and thorough news coverage. Perhaps in no other area have they been so successful and so unhampered by commitments to sponsors.

Television has received, and surely deserves, a great deal of criticism. Almost total commercial control of television programming is a very questionable basis on which to operate what is possibly the most potent single influence in American life. Yet it is too early to judge television or to understand it thoroughly. Our television critics, for example, are not yet as good as our film critics—an indication of the difficulties in coming to grips with this ever-present *but* MYSTERIOUS ELECTRONIC MIRACLE!

to make a film

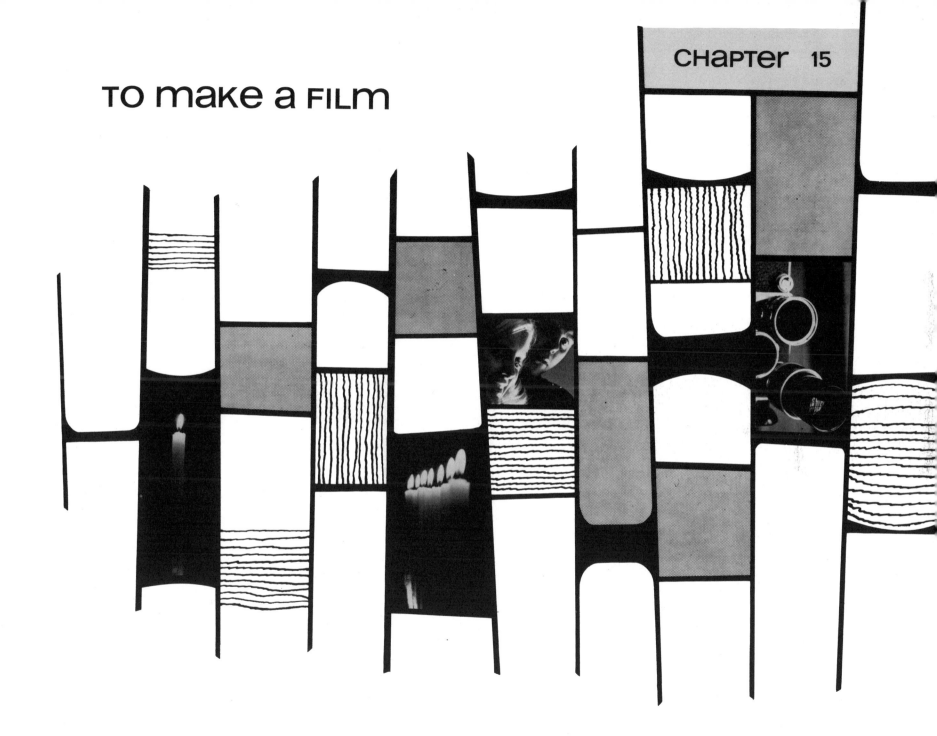

There can be no full understanding of film language until you have made a film. Something important happens when you hold a camera and then later watch the pictures you took flash on a screen — even if they are overexposed and badly edited. Perhaps it is like the difference between learning all about music and never actually singing, between learning all about effective speaking and never actually addressing a crowd. It is the difference between passively watching a film and comparing yourself with the film maker . . . his techniques with yours. Only the person who has used a movie camera can say as he watches another movie, "I wouldn't have done it that way." When you are capable of thinking in these terms, you are thinking in visual language.

The process that goes into the making of a film by amateurs is not terribly complex; nor are there really hard and fast "rules" on how to do it. This chapter offers suggestions which can be helpful.

The first step is a critical one: an idea. Students often get a kick out of imitating commercials or sometimes spoofing them. This chapter includes a storyboard prepared by some students

for a Volkswagen commercial "Moonshot." Although actual filming of such a commercial would be difficult, other commercials — for detergents, toothpastes, cigarettes — are easy to imitate or spoof. Or, try a commercial for a brand-new product (maybe brand X; nobody advertises brand X). The possibilities for humor and quick action are endless. The commercial as a form is easy to work with, because it is so short and has become so familiar. They offer much room for creative effort. A Benson and Hedges spoof began with the blackboard statement "The disadvantages of Benson and Hedges." Three students in a classroom at 3:30 checked the door and sneaked to the back of the room for a few puffs. Two students had regular-sized cigarettes; the other a Benson and Hedges. Time passed. The two finished their cigarettes; the other student was still puffing when a teacher passed. The teacher looked in, grabbed the guilty Benson and Hedges smoker—poor fellow! It is surprising what you can do in one minute or three minutes.

Storyboard for VW commercial "Moonshot"

Opening shot: long shot of rocket on pad
Sound: "four...three...two..one"

2.

Continued shot: rocket shoots upward
Sound: "BLAST OFF!"

3.
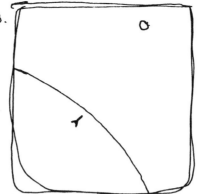

Long shot: rocket headed towards moon
Sound: rocket "whoosh"

4.
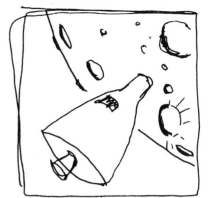

Near shot: from behind rocket; moon near
Sound: silent

5.

Establishing shot on moon: rocket drops slowly
Sound: landing gear whine

6.

Closer shot: rocket lands; dust stirred
Sound: "THUMP" of landing

7.

Shot: from undeneath rocket, orange doors begin to open
Sound: machinery openning doors

8.
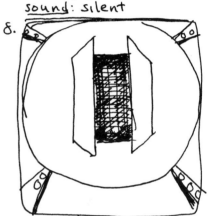

Continuing shot: as doors open, inside seems dark
Sound: machinery continues

9.

Continuing shot: doors open, elevator descends
Sound: door machinery stops, elevator sounds begin

10.
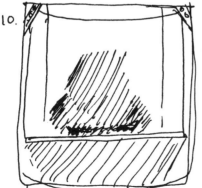

Shot: as object descends, camera dollies backward, slowly tilts, showing shadowy shape
Sound: elevator sounds stop

11.
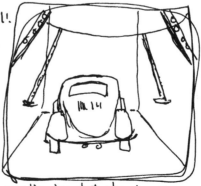

Continuing shot: showing rear view of Volkswagen!
Sound: engine starting
NARRATOR: "You've heard that Volkswagens will go anywhere on earth..."

12.
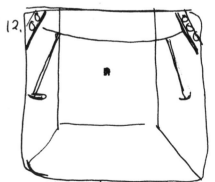

Continuation: car drives away
Sound: puttering of engine in distance
NARRATOR: "We at Volkswagen are known for our understatement."

But you needn't limit yourself to a commercial. Tell a story. "Supergoof," a four-minute film prepared by students, followed a superhero who constantly tripped over his beach-towel cape. Another described a bank robbery, followed by a gunfight among the robbers in which all of them were killed; the final shot was of a church sign "God watches over us." "Football Game," a simple film made at a neighborhood playground, depicted a Charlie Brown-type character winning all the games — not because he was good, but because everyone else was so bad.

Ideas can begin with a commercial, a story, or a technique. Some very fine student films have been created by shooting still pictures from magazines — say of the Vietnam war — then intercutting those with other pictures, to try to say something through the juxtaposition.

An idea, then, is the first step. The best resource for good ideas is a young imagination, and even better, a group of young imaginations brainstorming together.

The second step may be a more difficult one: getting a camera. Kodak claims that there are over eight million 8mm. cameras loose in the United States. And most of these are rather loose.

George and Harriet get married, receive a camera and projector as a gift, then let them sit in a closet for years. If George and Harriet happen to be your uncle and aunt, or better yet, your mother and father, you have it made. Home-movie equipment can be rented, usually by the day, and if several groups of students can do their shooting in one day, it's well worth it. Also, cameras can be bought for prices below $20 at pawnshops and auctions — though it is hard to judge how good they will be.

Begin by believing you can get a camera somewhere, and you will. It's best to choose 8mm. or Super-8 equipment — even if the school has a 16mm. camera (I recommend Super-8). The problem with 16mm. is expense: roughly three times the expense per foot of film for purchasing and developing. If you can afford it, great, otherwise, stick with 8mm. or Super-8. Remember that most 8mm. projectors will not handle Super-8, and vice versa.

So you have an idea and a camera; what now? Before you worry about the film, or the actors and props, remember, it is important to think out your idea visually — how you are going to handle it. A great aid here is the storyboard, a mock-up of the whole film, using sketches and descriptions to describe the action. "Moonshot," the suggested Volkswagen commercial, was created by a group of high school freshmen. The format used here gives you an indication of how a storyboard is prepared.

The storyboard is only one possible form of describing a planned film on paper. An older, and more frequently used form is the shooting script. The partial script from the National Film Board of Canada's production SELKIRK OF RED RIVER suggests the essential elements of the shooting script: camera placement, dialogue, movement, in effect all of the action and words to appear in the final film. The shooting script used in most Hollywood or network productions is generally a more thorough form.

CAMERON

Aye. Mongrels, he says. Half-Indian. Half-French.
And half black devil.

GRANT

All settlers to leave. Now! There will never be a
Red River colony.

SOME WOMEN AND CHILDREN BEGIN TO PASS THROUGH FRAME IN FEAR AND OBEDIENCE
TO GRANT.

MCDONALD

Lord Selkirk shall hear of this!

CAMERON

And will do nothing! A dandy -- a dreamer of dreams
who sits snug in Scotland.

GRANT CALLS. THEY LOOK OVER.

GRANT RIPS DOWN HUDSON'S BAY FLAG. HE CLAPS HIS HAND AND A LIGHTED TORCH
IS FLUNG INTO FRAME. HE CATCHES IT. HE SETS FIRE TO THE FLAG AND HURLS
IT TO CAMERA.

CUT TO: SERIES TITLE:

HISTORY MAKERS

FADE OUT

Scene FADE IN
B
1

EXT. CU. WOODEN SIGN SWINGS ON SIDE OF BUILDING -- (DAY) -- SNOWING.

Sign reads: "Maitland, Garden and Auldjo" "Montreal". As wind swings sign
toward camera:

SUPER: "SELKIRK OF RED RIVER"

CUT PAMPHLET IN SELKIRK'S HAND.

SELKIRK TOSSES PAMPHLET ONTO TABLE. SHOT WINDENS TO:

INT. OFFICE OF MAITLAND, GARDEN AND AULDJO. - (DAY) --

In the room are: LORD SELKIRK, DR. JOHN ALLAN, SAMUEL GALE, WILLIAM
MCGILLIVRAY AND ARCHIBALD NORMAN MCLEOD.

SELKIRK

Today I am an "unprincipled land-jobber."..And
I have sent my fellow Scots to Red River .. an
isolated desert to be massacred by savages! --

MCGILLIVRAY

Feelings run high in Montreal. Surely Your Lordship
is aware of what people are saying?

SELKIRK

That I have come to Montreal -- not to seek an amalgamation
between Hudson's Bay and the North West Company, but to
crush the North West Company .. I am also aware, Mr. McGillivray,
that our negotiations, conducted in "secrecy" miraculously become common street gossip!

Portion of a 1964 National Film Board of Canada film script, SELKIRK OF RED RIVER by William M. Altman

Not very often used, but helpful for suggesting the kinds of movement possible in a film, is the flip chart. Basically this is a pad of paper with individual, slightly different drawings on each sheet. When flipped by hand, these give the illusion of movement. Cartoons are flip charts transferred onto film, and it is very possible (although taxing on your patience) to make a cartoon this way. Use sheets of paper large enough for filming (4 by 6 inches is fine), and remember that in every second of 8mm. film you need 16 fresh drawings (24 per second in 16mm.). Your backgrounds needn't change each frame, only the figure doing the movement. Animation offers exciting possibilities, but remember that it is going to be work.

It is not necessary to make a storyboard or shooting script for your film. You may begin just shooting; but the final film will not reflect the care and precision which a storyboard, if carefully thought out and held to, would provide.

Now you are closing in: ready to make a film no one ever has attempted. Story line okay. Camera ready. Next: film, and action.

There is some knowledge involved in putting film in the camera and in preparing to shoot. The best place to get the "in" word on these details is from whatever source you get the camera. If your school has a photography club, someone there might be able to come around and help, explaining all the little dials and knobs and windows in the camera. Here, for whatever help they can be, are some basics.

Eight-millimeter cameras and Super-8 cameras are two different kinds of cameras. The *film* in Super-8 is the same size as 8, but the *frame* is larger and the sprocket holes are different. Super-8 is slightly more expensive, but is generally easier to work with, and the projected image is larger and brighter.

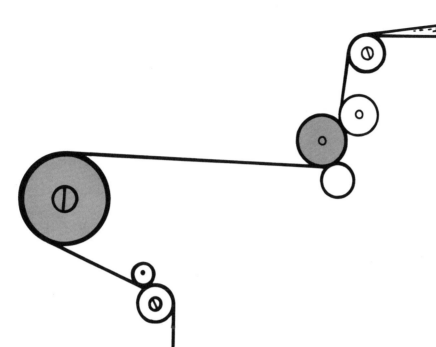

to decrease the speed so that the action appears to happen much faster than normally. If you change from a speed of 16 frames per second to 32 frames per second, you should open the lens diaphragm one stop (say from f-16 to f-11). If your camera has a built-in light meter (a plastic ridged surface above the lens) with automatic control of the f-stop, the camera usually does the work for you. Super-8 cameras adjust automatically. If not, you should make your own adjustments on the f-stop. If you have a light meter, that will help considerably in the adjustments. If not, here is a chart which can be helpful for basic kinds of *outdoor* light. This chart is based on Kodachrome II film with a speed of 25 ASA, 16 frames per second.

Daylight Exposure

Bright or hazy sun— in a light place	Bright or hazy sun— but distinct shadows*	Cloudy bright— no shadows	Heavy overcast	Open shade†
f/16	between f/11 and f/16	f/8	f/5.6	f/5.6

*For backlighted subjects, set lens at f/8.
†Use a filter to minimize the bluishness.

The lenses on most modern 8mm. and Super-8 cameras are "fixed focus." That means there is no need to focus them. Everything from about three feet away will be in focus when you shoot, provided the f-stop is set at f-8 or higher. The chart below provides the nearest shooting distance for use with the normal "fixed-focus" 8mm. movie camera:

Lens Setting	1.9 or 2	2.3	2.7 or 2.8	4	5.6	8	11	16
Distance In Feet	10	8½	8	6	4½	3½	2½	2

Eight-millimeter film usually comes on spools. Getting them inside the camera is easy enough. Super-8mm. film usually comes in magazine cartridges: like tape cartridges, you have only to slip the plastic box into the camera — no other work required. Sixteen-millimeter film usually comes in reels, or spools. Remember that 8mm. film is running through the lens at 16 frames per second; 16 mm. film at 24 frames per second. Timing, if you want to save film when you are shooting, sometimes has to be split second.

The devices on an 8mm. camera may be frightening at first, but are fairly simple. There is the button to turn the camera on and off, the "f-stop" to control the amount of light entering the camera, a focusing ring and, perhaps, a zoom lens.

Why do you need an f-stop control? For much the same reason that you need sunglasses at the beach. No matter what the weather when you're shooting, your aim is to keep a constant amount of light going through the lens to the film. So, on a bright day, you close down the f-stop from, say, f-8 to f-16. On a dull day, you open it up from f-8 to f-4.5. Just remember that the *lower* the f number, the *more* the light can get through to the film; the *higher* the f number, the *less* light will be admitted.

Another factor which affects the amount of light reaching the film is the speed at which the camera is running. Normal speed for silent movies is 16 frames per second. Some cameras allow you to increase the speed for slow-motion effects, or

The basic kinds of lenses are the regular lens (found on "fixed-focus" cameras), the wide-angle lens (which views a much wider area than the regular lens), and the long lens (also known as telephoto). The different effects of these different lenses can be seen opposite. Most shots can be taken satisfactorily with a regular lens, but the wide-angle lens can be very expressive in a closed space, and the telephoto lens can close in on things you can't get close to. It has the advantage, too, of throwing the background out of focus. A zoom lens combines the three basic lenses in one single variable lens, enabling you to "zoom in on the subject"—a sudden, often dramatic, visual jump from a scene to a particular object, or from a group of people to a single face.

The subjects and camera in these photos remained in a fixed position; only the lens was changed.

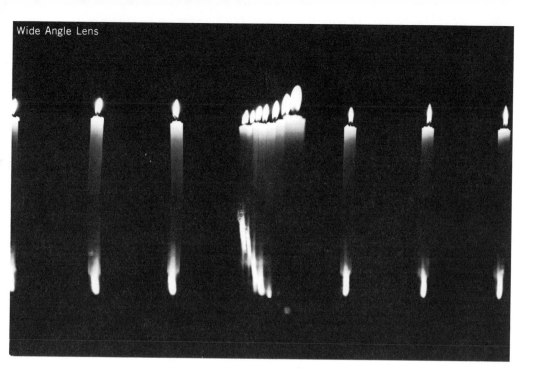

Wide Angle Lens

Such are some complexities of an 8mm. movie camera. Again, it is suggested that you contact someone in photography before shooting. There are enough mistakes possible that it would be good to keep the odds in your favor.

A couple of things about film: you have the choice of working in color or in black and white, and your decision should be based on what you intend to shoot. If it's all outdoor shooting, there's no problem with color. If it's indoors, you will need floodlights or perhaps even strobes (extra powerful indoor lights) for good color exposure. Generally, indoor shooting is best done with Tri-X black and white film, a high-speed variety which enables you generally to shoot with available indoor light. Tri-X is readily available in 16mm., 8mm., and Super-8mm.

If you decide to shoot in color, be sure to purchase either "indoor" or "daylight" color film. (The film prepared for indoor shooting contains special chemicals and will look pretty bad outdoors — and vice versa.)

So: Idea — Camera — Film. What next? If you are working in a team (best way to work: director, cameraman, actors, and anyone else you wish to recruit for the film), the actual shooting is fun. Make sure the cameraman has time to set up his camera. It's a good principle, by the way, to keep it propped on something more substantial than a palm. Cameras that jiggle as they shoot produce pictures that jiggle as they are projected. Some lively shooting can be done with the hand-held camera, but only if the cameraman has a steady hand.

You don't *have* to edit the film. You can shoot in the sequence that will enable you to show the film whole as it is returned from the labs. The problem here is that you don't give yourself room for error; and error is inevitable. It takes an expert to shoot a film sequence ready for projection. For best results, shoot a second or more before and after each scene (more than you need), and plan to edit it.

Set up your shots. Think where you want the camera (where it catches the action most effectively). Vary your shots, but not only for the sake of variety; let the story or the idea dictate the shot. It takes thought, but it's worth the effort. Remember that in a two-minute film, 15 seconds can be much too long for a shot. Remember also the general pattern of editing: long shot (to establish the *where*), medium shot, close-up. You needn't follow this every time, but this can serve as a standard. Again, let the story dictate.

Use close-ups as often as you can. Faces are the key to a good film about people. Your zoom lens, if you have one, can be most effective here.

Make sure that the light does not ruin your shots. To shoot when the sun is directly behind or in front of the camera creates a weaker image, generally, than when the light is coming from the side. At times this weaker image may be preferred — it depends on the idea you're attempting to convey. Filters — especially on bright days — can reduce glare and bring out special qualities in shots of the sky, grass, etc.

continuity or filmic disaster

Three important rules to keep in mind in preparing and shooting your film: clarity, comprehension, continuity. Clarity means an image which is sharp and clear. You can tell Roy from Archie. Jiggled cameras, out-of-focus shots, badly lit shots, or badly unlit shots ruin clarity. A sharp, crisp image encourages the viewer to concentrate on the screen. A blurred, sloppy image makes him wish he were doing something else.

Clarity requires technical skill and care; comprehension requires something more — thought. Know your story, and keep thinking of it in terms of the viewer sitting out there and watching it for the first time. If an actor is supposed to wait in an alley, use every shot to give him the semblance of waiting: lighting a cigarette or dropping a stub next to ten crushed stubs. Don't baffle the viewer by introducing irrelevant moments. Each shot should be taken with a comprehension of what it means for the *total* film.

Continuity requires skill and thought. Each film should move at its own pace, so there are few overall laws about continuity. But be sure you establish a pace (even though the pace itself may vary) and keep to it. If you jump from scene to scene, do it in such a way that the viewer can understand what is happening.

Any good film story, as you will recall from the chapter on editing, is not presented as a whole story — it is made up of fragments of action. We see only the important things: the gunman swaggering into the bar, the look on the bartender's face, the terrified features of the hunted man, the people backing away. The photographer only rarely needs to show the whole scene — if he can shoot the significant details (especially the faces) and edit these properly, the story will move with continuity and effectiveness. The key is to choose the right details. And to shoot them — this is important — in an order which will make sense to the viewer.

So you have shot the film: three minutes, say, from which you intend to extract 60 wild, vital seconds. Photography stores and many drugstores

will get your film to a developing lab and back to you within days, at most a week. Get a projector and view it. Watch it several times, to determine where and when you want to edit.

Your editing should be dominated by the way in which the shots are taken. In other words, shooting and editing are more properly parts of one process rather than two separate processes. The work of the editor usually is to select the best portions of each shot. Editing should preserve and assist continuity — not confuse the audience, but make it easier for the audience to follow. To have a man walking toward the left side of the screen and suddenly switch the camera position to have him walking toward the right side confuses the audience.

The physical work of editing is easy. A device called an "editor" helps. This is a combination of winding spools for the reels, set so the film goes into a lighting chamber which shines the image on a small screen, like a portable television set. Editors are available from camera shops for 8mm., Super-8, and 16mm. An editor is helpful. It may be too expensive to purchase, but ordinarily it can be rented. It is especially helpful with 8mm. and Super-8, where you have to squint hard to see the images on the film itself.

A splicer is also helpful, though not necessary. The splicer is often a part of the editor, and is usually attached to the base of it. A splicer simply cuts the film, and enables you to scrape the edges free of emulsion, apply splicing cement, and clamp the two end strips together quickly. Splicing tape (presstape) holds as well as most splicing cement, but the work is longer and more difficult — especially with tiny film like 8mm. All of these aids — editor, splicer, splicing cement, and presstapes — are available at local photography stores.

Once the editing is finished, the film is complete — or almost. If you plan to add sound, figure that you have a little more work (and expense) ahead. Generally, two ways of adding sound are available: optical tracks and magnetic tracks. In both cases film laboratories will have to do the actual work of putting the sound onto the film. Make sure, in either case, that your tape recording is sharp and clear. (If you use a magnetic stripe on an 8mm. or Super-8mm. film, be *sure* that you have a projector that picks up the sound.)

If you decide not to use sound, you can always revert to the method used by the earlier silent films: title cards. A blackboard, a large sheet of paper written up by a magic marker, even something like the configuration of Scrabble pieces, can serve as titles, which need only to be photographed and edited into the film. If you are working in color, you can make your titles colorful — one student used spaghetti dipped in food coloring. The same goes for opening and closing credits. Let your imagination be your guide.

There is really no more. Except to show the film. Remember that the size of the image you will get — and how far across the room you can throw the image — will depend on the film you have used. Sixteen-millimeter provides a much clearer, larger image than 8mm. or Super-8mm. And Super-8mm. projects a larger image than 8mm. Don't expect to show an 8mm. film to 500 people!

These remarks are a very rapid view of the work involved in making a movie. For a really well-made movie there is much, much more to be learned; but making a movie is the best way to learn. The important thing is that you make a movie: get a camera, film, and shoot. Everything after that is yours. Who knows? It can be ....

BIBLIOGraPHY for Chapter 15

British Film Institute, *Film Making in Schools and Colleges*. A brief, interesting treatment of the ways in which film making is being used at different levels of the curriculum in Britain.

Freytag, H., *Reinhold Photo and Movie Book*. New York: Reinhold Publishing Company, 1964. An excellent guide to the art of still photography and non-professional film making; lavishly illustrated.

Gaskill, Arthur L. with David A. Englander, *How to Shoot a Movie Story*. New York: Morgan and Morgan, Publishers, 1960. This book is subtitled, "The Technique of Pictorial Continuity." It describes the various techniques involved in movie making, but from the perspective of continuity. Excellent.

Kodak, editors of, *How to Make Good Home Movies*. Rochester, New York: Kodak (paperback; $1.25). Probably the most valuable brief treatment of the basics of amateur film making; goes into the camera, film lighting, setups, etc.; available only through camera stores.

MacGowan, Kenneth, *Behind the Screen, The History and Techniques of the Motion Picture*. New York: Dell Publishing Co., Inc., 1965. MacGowan's book is interesting; the first half of it describes the early history of film, up to the end of the silent era. The second half treats questions of censorship, the men behind the making of a movie, and the various new kinds of screens. The unevenness in structure is made up by MacGowan's relatively original approach to the intricate relationships between technique and psychological and artistic effects which undergirds the movies.

Spottiswoode, Raymond, *A Grammar of the Film*. Berkeley: University of California Press, 1962 (paperback). Originally written in the 1930's, this book is very dated; but many of the terms and descriptions can still be useful.

Film and Its Techniques. Berkeley: University of California Press, 1966. Written in 1950, this book is also dated, but not nearly so much as *Grammar*. Probably the best overall book to the equipment and process of movie making.

Sullivan, Sister Bede, *Movies, The Universal Language*. South Bend, Indiana: Fides Press, 1967 (paperback). Sister Bede Sullivan has taught movies to youngsters — all ages — for a number of years, and this book records many of her most effective experiences. Her suggestions on student film making are especially valuable.